Trust and Obey

(Obedience and the Christian)

R. C. Sproul
Michael Horton
John MacArthur
John Armstrong
Jonathan Gerstner
Joel Beeke
Ray Lanning

Edited by Rev. Don Kistler

Soli Deo Gloria

. . . for instruction in righteousness . . .

Soli Deo Gloria Publications
P.O. Box 451, Morgan, PA 15064
(412) 221-1901/FAX 221-1902

*

*

ISBN 1-57358-057-0

Contents

The Authors

Dr. R. C. Sproul is founder and Chairman of Ligonier Ministries of Orlando, Florida. He studied under the late Dr. John H. Gerstner at Pittsburgh Theological Seminary and holds a degree from the Free University of Amsterdam. He is an ordained minister in the Presbyterian Church of America, in addition to being Distinguished Visiting Professor of Systematic Theology and Apologetics at Knox Theological Seminary in Ft. Lauderdale, Florida. Dr. Sproul is in constant demand as a speaker and author. He has authored many books, among them *The Holiness of God, Chosen by God, Abortion: A Rational Look at an Emotional Issue,* and *Knowing Scripture.* He was a contributing author to *Justification by Faith ALONE!* and *Sola Scriptura.*

Dr. Michael Horton is the President of Christians United for Reformation. He is a graduate of Biola University, and of Westminster Theological Seminary in California, and he completed his doctoral work at Wycliffe Hall, Oxford. A prolific author, he has written or edited *Putting Amazing Back Into Grace, The Agony of Deceit, Beyond Culture Wars, The Law of Perfect Freedom,* and

Power Religion. His latest project, available at bookstores or through CURE, is titled *In the Face of God: The Dangers and Delights of Spiritual Intimacy.* He is ordained in the Christian Reformed Church and is currently a Research Fellow at Yale University.

Dr. John MacArthur is pastor/teacher at Grace Community Church in Sun Valley, California. A graduate of Talbot Theological Seminary, he can be heard daily throughout the country on his radio program, "Grace To You." He is the author of numerous bestsellers, including: *The Gospel According to Jesus, The Vanishing Conscience, Faith Works, Charismatic Chaos,* and his new book on discernment, *Reckless Faith.* Dr. Mac-Arthur also serves as President of the Master's College and Seminary in Southern California. He was a contributing author to *Justification by Faith ALONE!* and *Sola Scriptura.*

Dr. John Armstrong is the Director of Reformation & Revival Ministries, and editor of *Reformation & Revival Journal*, a theological quarterly for church leadership. He received his B.A. degree from Wheaton College, an M.A. degree from the Wheaton College Graduate School of Theology, and his D.Min. degree from Luther

Rice Seminary, Atlanta, Georgia. He is the general editor of *Roman Catholicism: Evangelical Protestants Analyze What Unites and Divides Us* (Moody Press, 1994) and author *Can Fallen Pastors Be Restored?* (Moody Press, 1995). Before entering his present ministry he served as a Baptist minister for 21 years. He was a contributing author to *Justification by Faith ALONE!* and *Sola Scriptura.*

Dr. Jonathan Gerstner is Professor of Apologetics and Church History at Knox Theological Seminary in Fort Lauderdale, Florida. He received a Ph.D. from the University of Chicago in theology, and has also done graduate study at the University of Utrecht in the Netherlands and the University of Stellensboch in the Republic of South Africa. He is the author of *The Thousand-Generation Covenant: Dutch Reformed Covenant Theology and Group Identity in Colonial South Africa from 1652 to 1814.* He has served as Professor of Systematic and Practical Theology at Payne Theological Seminary in Wilberforce, Ohio (the oldest African-American seminary) and as Executive Secretary of the Reformed Church in Canada (where he was a denominational spokesman and consultant in new church development and church revitalization. He is the son of the late Dr. John H. Gerstner and the author Edna Gerstner.

Dr. Joel Beeke is the pastor of Heritage Netherlands Reformed Congregation of Grand Rapids, Michigan, and President and Professor of Systematic Theology at Puritan Reformed Theological Seminary. He earned a Ph.D. in Reformation and Post-Reformation Theology from Westminster Theological Seminary in Philadelphia. He is the author of several books, including *Assurance of Faith: Calvin, English Puritanism, and the Dutch Second Reformation*. Dr. Beeke is also editor of *The Banner of Sovereign Grace Truth* magazine, President of Reformation Heritage Books, and radio pastor for "The Gospel Trumpet." He was a contributing author to *Justification by Faith ALONE!* and *Sola Scriptura*.

Rev. Ray Lanning is pastor of the Independent Reformed Church of Cutlerville in Grand Rapids, Michigan. He is a graduate of Westminster Theological Seminary and has done graduate work at Calvin Theological Seminary. Ordained to the ministry in 1977, he has served Presbyterian and Reformed churches in various parts of the U.S. and Canada.

Introduction

We live in a pragmatic age. We no longer ask "Is it true?" but, rather, "Does it work?" The emphasis on pragmatic experientialism has fostered a confusion that has infiltrated the church, manifested by placing the personal "What do I get from it?" ahead of the more scriptural "What am I going to do about it?" The articles in this book do not deal with what man gets, but rather with who God is and what He has done, does, and will do to position the individual to glorify and enjoy Him forever. Thus, the critical question becomes "What am I going to do about what God has done?" The issue is obedience.

Love for God, by regeneration implanted in the heart of a sinner, is possessed by everyone who is born from above and in a justified state (Ezekiel 36:26-27). God does for us in our sinfulness what we could not do in our righteousness—He gives us the principle and the power to obey. Love for God becomes the grand principle and source of all acceptable obedience, and the Spirit is the everpresent power to help us fulfill the obedience which Scripture so expressly requires in order to attain the enjoyment of God.

"If you love me you will keep My commandments. And I will give you another Helper, that
He may be with you forever; that is, the Spirit of
truth" (John 14:15–17a). The words of Jesus explicitly state that both holiness of heart (love)
and holiness of conduct (obedience) are absolutely necessary to give evidence of one's confession of faith. The essence of obedience lies in
the hearty love which prompts the act rather
than the act itself. It is not so much what we are
doing or saying, but what our heart is meaning
and intending—though what our heart is meaning and intending is *usually* seen in what we are
doing or saying. By obedience to the commands
of God, we give evidence of our holy conversion.
By this our faith is declared genuine before the
world. Who-ever pretends to believe in Jesus and
is not habitually careful to be obedient, his faith,
as manifested by his lack of works, is worthless,
barren, dead. By walking in the paths of duty, we
express our gratitude to God for His gracious
benefits and also glorify His holy name, which is
the great aim of all obedience (Matthew 5:16).

It must be stated that neither our external
obedience nor our internal holiness constitutes
any part of the righteousness by which we are
justified (declared righteous before God). Nor is
either of those the cause or condition of our ac-

ceptance with God. That righteousness by which we are justified must be absolutely perfect (see our book *Justification by Faith ALONE!*). Thus Paul, the great teacher of the Gentiles, when considering that he would stand before the tribunal of God, declared his hope that he "may be found in Him, not having a righteousness of my own derived from the Law, but that which is through faith in Christ, the righteousness which comes from God on the basis of faith" (Philippians 3:9). That righteousness which was wrought out before we were born is the only ground by which our final Judge can discharge our guilt. If anyone should ask, "How shall I appear before God and be found right?" the answer is: Trust in the obedience of Christ. If the question should be, "How can I express my gratitude to God for His gracious mercy to me?" the answer is: Obey the commands of Christ and live in conformity to His revealed will.

It is our intention as publishers of this work to remind the church of the propriety of good works. As previously stated, though our works of obedience are of no consideration in procuring justification, or in obtaining a title to eternal life, they are most important in offsetting those fatal and opposite extremes, legalism and antinomian licentiousness. The former infringes on the glory of grace, exalts self, and wounds our peace. The latter turns the grace of God into wantonness, hardens our conscience, and renders us worse than unbelievers. The notable authors in this work have joined us in exhorting the Lord's sheep to rightly distinguish between the foundation of our acceptance with God (justification) and the superstructure of practical godliness (sanctification).

The sagacious Puritan John Owen, some centuries ago, wrote on Psalm 130: "Our foundation in dealing with God is Christ alone, mere grace and pardon in Him. Our building is in and by holiness and obedience, as the fruits of that faith by which we have received the atonement."

The principle that underlies this book is that love is the foundation of obedience, and that obedience is the sure outcome and result of love. Other foundation can no man lay than on Jesus Christ to trust and obey. *Soli Deo Gloria!*

Dr. Bruce Bickel
Chairman of the Board, Soli Deo Gloria

John Bishop   Rev. Don Kistler
Millersville, MD   *Pittsburgh, PA*

Peter Neumeier   Rev. Lance Quinn
Atlanta, GA   *Little Rock, AR*

Oh, How I Love Thy Law!

R. C. Sproul

When we think of the Beatitudes we immediately think of the Sermon on the Mount. In terms of the redemptive historical setting we think of course of the New Testament. The Beatitudes have to do with the teaching of Jesus, and the form that Jesus used in giving the Beatitudes was a throwback to Old Testament Israel—the adaptation of a prophetic mode of communication that used, as its conveyance, the oracle.

In pagan religion, the oracle was viewed as a form of communication from God, as was the case of the oracle of Delphi. It was a divine announcement, a *pronouncement* that could be either positive or negative. Positively it could proclaim prosperity to a person or to a nation; negatively it was an announcement of divine judgment that proclaimed an impending, ominous doom—such as that which is declared in the book of Revelation when we read in the last times of the angel that appeared, crying through the heavens, "Woe, Woe, Woe." That is

an oracle of judgment. It is the kind of oracle
Jesus pronounced upon the Pharisees of His
day. But the oracle of weal, the divine announcement of benediction, God's declaration
of felicity, was couched in the oracle of blessing.

The word "blessing" has been almost emp-
tied of its biblical meaning. It cheapens blessing
to refer to it as simply as an experience of
happiness. To be blessed, in the Hebrew mind,
was to be filled in one's soul with the capacity
to experience the loveliness, the excellence, and
the sweetness of God Himself. The word "happiness" falls short of this. Even "fulfillment"
falls short. Indeed, it involves a filling, a full-
ness, an abundance of joy and peace and
stability. The Jew longed for the day when he
would hear God give His benediction. The
people were stirred when they listened to their
Messiah declare unto them, "Blessed are those
who are poor. Blessed are those who mourn, for
they shall be comforted. Blessed are those who
hunger and thirst after righteousness, for they
will be filled. Blessed are the peacemakers, for
they will be called the children of God."

We tend to restrict our understanding of the
Beatitudes to the New Testament when, in reality, the concept of beatitude, of a beatific experience, is rooted and grounded in the Old

Testament. We sometimes sing one of the rich-
est beatitudes of all of Scripture: the beatitude
that introduces the Psalter. This first song is a
beatitude, a benediction. It is not a concluding
benediction in the sense of a message that
comes at the end of worship, but manifests the
original meaning of "benediction"—a good saying, a divine announcement of blessedness.
Psalm 1 reads: "Blessed is the man that walketh
not in the counsel of the ungodly, nor standeth
in the way of sinners, nor sitteth in the seat of
the scornful." The Psalm uses the poetic form
of parallelism that builds to a climax. The first
thing that is said of this blessed person is that
he does not walk in the counsel of the ungodly.
He is deaf to the advice of the pagan who elicits
our participation in the fads of this world.

In the first chapter of Romans, Paul expresses the degree of depravity into which this
world has fallen, the headlong plunge of mankind into heinous sin that is marked by a re-
fusal to honor God and to be grateful. He then
goes on to give a catalog of the sins familiar to
the human heart and race.

Paul writes, "And even as they did not like
to retain God in their knowledge, God gave
them over to a reprobate mind, to do those
things which are not convenient; being filled

with all unrighteousness, fornication, wicked-
ness, covetousness, maliciousness; full of envy,
murder, debate, deceit, malignity; whisperers,
backbiters, haters of God, despiteful, proud,
boasters, inventors of evil things, disobedient to
parents, without understanding, covenant-
breakers, without natural affection, implacable,
unmerciful."

This short list of the characteristics of godlessness reaches its nadir in verse 32: "Who
knowing the judgment of God, that they which
commit such things are worthy of death, not
only do them but have pleasure in them that do
them."

Paul says that our sinful inclinations are so
intense that not only do we do those things
which God prohibits, but we encourage other
people to do them with us.

Somehow we have the idea that our sin will
not be seen as sin if we can get enough people
to participate with us. But blessed is the man
who doesn't walk according to that kind of
counsel, who doesn't walk in the counsel of the
ungodly, who doesn't stand in the way of sinners. That does not mean that the person is
blessed who doesn't get in front of sinners and
obstruct their ability to move. That is not what
it means to "stand in the way of." This is ar-

chaic language. It means the person who does not stand in the road of sinners, who doesn't participate in the godlessness of the wicked. Blessed is that person, and the one who doesn't sit in the seat of the scornful.

The cheapest form of intellectual recognition a person who is not deep in intellectual analysis can have, the quick and dirty way to fraudulent intellectual respectability, is the way of cynicism. Anyone can be a cynic. And there is no worse kind of cynicism than the cynicism that enjoys scoffing at a human being's pursuit of godliness. The Psalmist tells us that blessed is the man who doesn't sit in that seat. The opposite is implied elliptically: "Cursed is the man who does." But you notice that up to this point in the Psalm, the beatitude is describing a person in negative terms. That is, the blessedness comes to a person who doesn't do these things just mentioned.

What *does* he do? What characterizes the blessed person? "But his delight is in the law of the Lord, and in that law doth he meditate day and night." It's not just "blessed is the man who doesn't do this," but "blessed is the one whose delight is in the law of the Lord." I am taking time on this because if there is anything that does *not* characterize the contemporary

church, anything that does *not* capture the
spirit of 20th-century so-called "evangelicalism," it is a pervasive, widespread delight in the
law of God. I know there are people reading
this saying, "Are you crazy? Where have you
been? Don't you know that we live on this side
of the cross? The law has been set aside. We're
Christians. We don't sit around and delight in
the law of God."

If you are a Christian, you do. And if you do
not delight in the law of God, don't deceive
yourself into thinking that you are a regenerate
person. Don't think that the gospel which frees
you from the curse of the law is a license for
you to despise the law or to ignore the law.
This pronouncement of blessedness is as appli-
cable today as it was when it was written. I
know we don't talk that way, but it is true
nonetheless.

Psalm 119 is one of the most magnificent
pieces of literature in the whole Old Testament.
It is a unparalled panegyric of the sweetness of
the law of God. And it follows in poetic mea-
sure the Hebrew alphabet. I call your attention
to Psalm 119:97 where we read these words:
"Oh, how I love Thy law."

Do you see what the Psalmist is saying? The
person who wrote this is part of the commu-

nion of saints. The person who wrote these words is part of the household of God. The person who wrote these words is an Old Testament saint. The person who wrote these words wrote them under the inspiration of God the Holy Spirit. And here is an ejaculation of religious affection, an unrestrained outburst of emotion. The Holy Spirit, we are told in the New Testament, causes us at times to groan. I can imagine the Psalmist groaning when he wrote these words. "Oh, how I love Thy law!" When was the last time you heard a Christian pour out his heart with affection for the law of God? How foreign that is to us!

What is he in love with and why is he in love? What is he speaking of when he speaks of this law that he loves so desperately, and why does he love it?

In the Old Testament and in the New, the Scriptures frequently make a distinction between law and gospel and a distinction between law and prophets. There are times when the word "law" is used in a general and broad sense. At other times, when it is contrasted with other dimensions, it takes on a more specified, narrow meaning. Sometimes it strictly refers to the commandments delivered by Moses or to the holiness code. But one of the most significant usages of the concept of "law" in the Old Testament is the generic sense of the law of God, referring indiscriminately to the Word of God, because the law of God is the Word of God and the Word of God is the law of God. The gospel is the Word of God, and the Word of God cannot be broken. Even the word of promise carries the force of law when it is uttered by God.

In the Hollywood version of "The King and I," the King of Siam often repeated the statement, "So let it be written; so let it be done." Everyone in Siam took the King's word as law (except Anna). But the godly person stands in awe at every word that comes from the mouth of God. Jesus called it His meat and drink. And to resist Satan and the forces of hell themselves, He said, "It is written, Man shall not live by bread alone but by every word that proceedeth forth from the mouth of God." He said that Scripture cannot be broken.

"Blessed is the man whose delight is in the Word of God, and in that Word does he, from time to time, look." Is that how it goes? No.

Is it "Blessed is the man who studiously applies himself to the Bible for five minutes a day"? No.

The blessed man is the one who meditates

day and night on God's law.

I ask the question again: Why does he love it? Look at Psalm 119:89–91: "Forever, O Lord, Thy Word is settled in heaven. Thy faithfulness is unto all generations. Thou hast established the earth and it abides. They continue this day according to Thine ordinances. For all are Thy servants."

The mores, the taboos, the customs of every human culture change from generation to generation. In 1950 not 1 percent of the people in America would condone abortion on demand. It was considered vice of the worst sort. We live on this side of the moral revolution of the 60s, in which virtue and vice shifted, but the Psalmist loved the law of God, and he loved the Word of God because His Word is settled.

I often mention my reaction to that oft-repeated phrase: "God says it. I believe it. That settles it." This sentiment borders on blasphemy. If it is going to be a truly Christian statement we must say: "God said it, that settles it." It doesn't matter whether we believe it or not. If it is God's Word, it's settled. This is what the Psalmist understood and he says it has been settled in heaven from eternity.

I talk to Christians who struggle with the state of their soul, who lack the assurance of salvation, and I tell them, "The Scriptures make it a priority for us to make our election sure. Get it settled." I do this because our consistency as Christians is bound up with how settled we are in our faith. The unsettled person is the double-minded person, the person who is unstable in all his ways and is tossed to and fro with every wind of doctrine. That is not what the Psalmist wants. The Psalmist wants an anchor for his soul, and the Psalmist loves that which settles it for him. "Oh, how I love Thy law because it is settled in heaven! And it endures for all generations!"

How did Mary say it? She rejoiced in a tradition that transmitted the promises of God from one generation to the next. It was a promise that was first made to Adam and Eve, a promise that was renewed to Abraham, to Isaac, and to Jacob of the One who would come and crush the head of the serpent. He would redeem His people.

After millennia passed, finally in a peasant village, without any warning, a visitor from the presence of God Himself named Gabriel appeared to this peasant girl and said, "The Lord is with you." As she absorbed the announcement, under the impetus of the Holy Spirit she cried out, "My soul doth magnify the Lord. My spirit doth rejoice in God my Savior, for He has noticed the low estate of his handmaiden, and from henceforth, all generations shall call me blessed." Then she went on to say, "He has remembered the promise that He made to our father Abraham." His Word continues to all generations.

Scholars in the past used to think that when they were studying science, they were studying the invisible hand of Providence. Isaac Newton believed that he was thinking God's thoughts after Him. The laws of nature were seen to be the evidence of His handiwork. Now, in human arrogance, we seek laws without a Lawgiver and despise the law of God. The Psalmist said, "Unless Thy law had been my delight I would have perished in my affliction." Why else?

Psalm 119:105 says, "Thy Word is a lamp unto my feet and a light unto my path."

It was my job as a young boy to run to the store and get the loaf of bread, to pick up the order my mother had called in, or to go to the drugstore at night and get the prescriptions for the family. I loved to go to the drugstore at night to dawdle at the soda fountain, but, once the sun had gone down, it was never without fear and trepidation, because to get to the store I had to go through Green's orchard. For a young boy, that was one of the scariest places in western Pennsylvania. There was a narrow path through the orchard lined by trees, one of which was a huge oak tree. In the dead of winter, when its branches stuck out into the starry night, it looked as if it had huge arms that would come down and grab any little kid who ran through that orchard. I was terrified to go to the store after dark. I did it a thousand times, but every time I approached that orchard it was like going to a graveyard. What I wanted was a full moon, a flashlight, a lamp unto my feet, a light for my path.

The tree never hurt me and it never grabbed me. But I have seen more just like it in this world, and I still need a lamp and I still need a light. "Oh, how I love Thy law," because the law of God is a mirror and reflection of His holiness and His excellence. John Calvin understood its importance for the New Testament Christian clearly when he discussed his third use of the law, its revelatory character—that the law of God reveals to us what is pleasing in His sight. When a Christian says, "I don't have to pay any attention to the law," I ask them immediately, "Do you have to pay attention to living a life that is pleasing to God?"

I once spoke at a conference in New York on

"The Holiness of God." I agreed to go to one of the homes after the evening service for a time of prayer with about twenty other people. After refreshments they said, "Let's have our time of prayer." They turned the lights off and suddenly started praying to their dead relatives.

I said, "Just a minute! What is this?"

They said, "This is a Spirit-led prayer and the Spirit has enabled us to make contact . . ."

I queried, "Do you know what the Bible says about this? Do you realize that in the Old Testament this was a capital offense? God calls this kind of behavior an abomination in His sight for which, if it goes unpunished, He will curse an entire nation."

They said, "Yes, we know that. But that is the Old Testament. Don't get hung up in the law, R. C."

I replied, "What has happened in the history of redemption that has taken a behavioral practice that was utterly repugnant to God in the Old Testament and has now made it something that pleases Him? A cursory reading of the Old Testament and a cursory understanding of the law of God would inform you immediately that this is something that God hates." We Christians are to look even to the Old Testament law to learn what is pleasing and sweet to God.

The Psalmist loved the law of God. Read again what he wrote: "Oh, how I love the law!" Is that what he said? What did I change? It's "Thy" law. We must not move from the personal to the impersonal, to a list of abstract rules and regulations. Nobody in Israel was falling in love with rules. It was "Oh, how I love *Thy* law!"

They loved the law because they understood that the law revealed Him whose law it is. If you love Him, then obviously you want to live a life that is pleasing to Him. You want to understand what He says is virtue. You love the law because it is *His* law, because you love the Lawgiver. How can you love God and hate His law? This is what Jesus said: "If you love Me, keep My commandments."

Psalm 119:140 says, "Thy Word is very pure; therefore Thy servant loveth it."

"Oh, how I love Thy law!" There is no dross in it; there is no error in it; it is pure and undefiled. Everything else, all of the counsel, all of the insight, all of the opinions of men that I have ever examined are flawed. There is not that sterling quality of essential purity, but "Thy Word is very pure; therefore I love it."

"Purity" is a word that has all but disappeared from our language. Where are today's

Puritans who want the pure gospel, the pure truth, the pure life of obedience? Where are those who seek the favor of God above all other considerations?

Finally, in Psalm 119:142 we read: "Thy righteousness is an everlasting righteousness, and Thy law is the truth." Christ was standing before Pontius Pilate who was there to judge Him. Pilate said, "I understand it has been said that you are a king. Is that right? Are you a king?"

Jesus answered, "Pilate, My kingdom is not of this world. If it were, My servants would rise up. But for this reason was I sent into this world, for this cause did I come: to bear witness to the truth. Everyone who is of the truth hears My voice."

When He was on trial for His life, Jesus, in the most succinct terms He could possibly use to define the essence of His mission, His reason for coming, chose to describe it in this way: "I came to bear witness to the truth." We are living in a church today that cares less about truth than any about other commodity. A love for the truth is not even a virtue; it's a vice, because truth divides people. Truth causes controversy. Truth causes debate. Truth upsets relationships. Truth gets people crucified. Jesus said, "Everyone who is of the truth hears My voice."

"Oh, how I love Thy law," because "Thy Word is truth." The man who wrote these words was like a tree planted by rivers of living water whose fruit would not wither, who would bring forth its fruit in its season. But "the ungodly are not so. They are like the chaff which the wind driveth away."

The chapters in this book strive to show what it means for Christians to love the law of God. To love the law of God is to love God. Every true Christian must love God. And, since to love God is to keep (and love) His commandments, then every true Christian *must* say, with the Psalmist, "Oh, how I love Thy law!"

Filthy Rags or Perfect Righteousness?

Michael Horton

One might have thought that the biblical writers were bankers, lawyers, and tailors by the frequency of the analogies and metaphors they used in describing God's saving work. Believers are "credited" with the righteousness and obedience of Christ, as the first Adam's "debts" had been "imputed" to their account. Or, in the spirit of the lawyer, Scripture labors in both testaments to make the point that sin is a legal transgression that requires perfect justice, and that the propitiatory sacrifice of Christ answers that dilemma. Believers are therefore "declared righteous" in a courtroom.

But it is that third trade (the tailor's) that provides the rich world of metaphors for the assignment of this chapter.

Wearing Someone Else's Clothes

The clothing metaphor appears in the Bible's opening pages. In their innocence, of course, Adam and Eve were perfectly satisfied with their natural constitution. After all, God had pronounced them "good," and that had reference not merely to their moral excellence, but to their physical beauty. Hardly an object of shame and disgrace, the human body was more splendid than Solomon's temple. Then came the infamous revolt. After realizing that instead of being enlightened they were naked and ashamed, they turned to their own resources: "Then the eyes of both of them were opened, and they realized they were naked; so they sewed fig leaves together and made coverings for themselves" (Genesis 3:7).

Aware of their lost condition, our first parents had no idea how to repair the situation. All they could see were externals, symptoms of the crisis; hence the fig leaves. The creation of this homespun covering, however, did not actually solve the inner conflict, so Adam and Eve fled to the forest from the presence of the One whose nearness had before always been a delight. God found the couple and brought them face to face with their real problem. It was not merely that they were naked, nor even that they were ashamed. People can feel ashamed without being guilty, but this was different. So God prosecuted His judgment. The law went to work, reading the record and pronouncing a sentence.

If this were the only word that God's speech contained, it would end in the total ruin of the human race; and God was not bound to utter any other word. Nevertheless, He freely chose to follow the judgment with justification, the sentence with salvation. In the midst of these terrible curses is the *proto-evangelion*, the first announcement of the gospel: "And I will put enmity between you and the woman," God tells the serpent, "and between your offspring and hers; he will crush your head, and you will strike his heel" (Genesis 3:15).

As the fig leaves had symbolized self-justification, this evangelical announcement is followed by new clothes: "The LORD God made garments of skin for Adam and his wife and clothed them" (v. 21). It is of eternal significance that what justified Adam and Eve (covered the devastating effects of their sins) was not something God did *in* them, but what He did *for* them, what He put *on* them.

When God made His covenant with Abraham, the patriarch believed and was justified (Genesis 15:6). In spite of Abraham's unfaithfulness, and that of his sons, God's covenant of

grace proceeds in its course. God is the only
hero of these stories. After Jacob's strange
wrestling match with the theophanic Lord, he
finally made his successful return to Bethel
where God had appeared to him in a dream,
promising to save Jacob according to His unconditional oath. And Jacob's response, now as
a believer instead of as a schemer, was to command his whole household to "get rid of the
foreign gods you have with you, and purify
yourselves and change your *clothes*" (Genesis
35:2). Then they came with him to the altar at
Bethel and worshipped God there through the
substitutionary sacrifice. Just as God had replaced the fig leaves of our first parents with
the royal garments of a sacrificial animal, so the
newly clothed Israel could only enter safely
into God's presence dressed in perfect righteousness.

Throughout the Old Testament, God's act of
clothing His sinful people in His own righteousness is a recurring theme. Job cries out, "I
put on righteousness as my clothing" (Job
29:14). The Psalmist rejoices, "You turned my
wailing into dancing; you removed my sack-
cloth and clothed me with joy" (Psalm 30:11).
"I delight greatly in the LORD," exults Isaiah.

"My soul rejoices in my God. For He has clothed me with garments of salvation and arrayed me in a robe of righteousness, as a bridegroom adorns his head like a priest, and as a bride adorns herself with her jewels" (Isaiah 61:10). Apart from this royal clothing, the sinner's case is hopeless: "Our righteous acts are like filthy rags" (Isaiah 64:6). Note that it is not merely our acts of disobedience, but "our *righteous* acts" that are so described.

A particularly striking scene is found in Zechariah:

> Then he showed me Joshua the high priest standing before the angel of the LORD, and Satan standing at his right side to accuse him. The LORD said to Satan, "The LORD rebuke you, Satan! The LORD, who has chosen Jerusalem, rebuke you! Is not this man a burning stick snatched from the fire?" Now Joshua was dressed in filthy clothes as he stood before the angel. The angels said to those who were standing before him, "Take off his filthy clothes." Then he said to Joshua, "See, I have taken away your sin, and I will put rich garments on you." Then I said, "Put a clean turban on his head." So they put a clean turban on his head and

> clothed him, while the angel of the LORD
> stood by (Zechariah 3:1–5).

Given the frequent appearances of "the angel of the LORD" in contexts where it is difficult to imagine this being merely one of the heavenly messengers, one might safely conclude that this is a reference to the preincarnate Son. This also makes sense in the light of further revelation, as the heavenly courtroom consists of the Judge, the prosecuting attorney (Satan), and the Defense Attorney (Jesus). It is this Angel of the LORD who commands his servants to strip Joshua of his filthy clothes and to clothe him in perfect righteousness. Only in this way can his sins be covered. Let us remember that Joshua was Israel's high priest, the one man who was allowed to enter annually into the Holy of Holies with the sacrifice for the people. Nevertheless, he is dressed in "filthy rags" until he is clothed with garments of salvation.

But these images are carried forward into their New Testament fulfillment. We are astonished by the graciousness of the father accepting his prodigal son who had squandered his inheritance on prostitutes in a far country. Willing to return as a servant and no longer a son in his father's house, the son was instead met with pure mercy. Although the prodigal confesses his unworthiness even to be called a son, the father commands his servants to act: "Quick! Bring the best robe and put it on him. Put a ring on his finger and sandals on his feet. Let's have a feast and celebrate" (Luke 15:22). In the parable of the wedding banquet, Jesus compares His work to that of a king who sent his servants to the streets to invite guests to the festive reception. "But when the king came in to see the guests, he noticed a man there who was not wearing wedding clothes." Like God asking Adam how he knew he was naked, the king asks this gentleman, "Friend, how did you get in here without wedding clothes?" Speechless, the man is thrown into outer darkness (Matthew 22:1–14).

It is in Paul's epistles that this image is especially emphasized. "Clothe yourselves with the Lord Jesus" (Romans 13:14). "You are all sons of God through faith in Christ Jesus, for all of you who were baptized into Christ have clothed yourselves with Christ" (Galatians 3:26–27). As the Bible begins with this rich imagery, so it ends, with the saints robed in white garments and clothed in Christ's victory

(Revelation 3:18; 6:11).

Perhaps the greatest evidence of our sinful nature is not found in horrible acts of immorality, violence, or selfish ambition, but in the fact that even when God offers us the wedding garment of a perfect righteousness we persist in our self-vindication! Whatever the fig leaves, whether made of self-esteem therapy or of energetic moralism, we refuse to see our filthy rags as insufficient to appear in the presence of a holy God. As one grand old Puritan said, "We attempt to cover filth with filth."

But most readers of this volume will not be among the vast body of men and women today who refuse the gospel of free grace. The doctrine of justification will not be the problem for most readers of a book like this one; but the practical enjoyment of it in the Christian life is another matter. A book on the relation of faith to obedience is not only likely to spur us on to greater faithfulness; it will drive some to utter despair. But this is the effect that such thoughts should have on all of us. Not only do we need to hear the calls to faithfulness again and again because we are slow to hear and obey; we need to hear them as the divine sentence on even our best works as Christians! Augustus

Toplady was quite right when he lamented that the best things he ever did in his life deserved damnation.

We hear serious calls to trust and obey, but before long (sinners that we still are) either we begin to think that our faith and commitment are perfect ("perfect submission," "absolute surrender," "victory," etc.), or a more accurate assessment leads us to doubt our salvation because of the weakness of our faith and repentance. It is in just these moments that we are startled by a fresh sense of our depravity that gripped us at first, and it is that sense that drives us once more to our perfect Savior whose undiminishable righteousness we wear. Our weak faith and the corruption clinging to our best works cannot *condemn*, because the strength of our faith and the purity of our actions cannot *save*. Even faith cannot save, but can only reach out, empty-handed, to receive the obedience and merit of a perfect Savior.

This is an important point, for, even where many evangelicals have resisted the obvious distortions and departures, there is a tendency to incorporate a subtle form of works-righteousness into the concept of faith itself. It is essential that we not view faith as something going out from us that somehow possesses a quality that substitutes for other, perhaps more difficult, works. Faith is not itself a virtue at all. It is, in the matter of justification, a *receiving* instrument and not a *giving* instrument. While this faith produces good works, it is not itself a good work that serves as the basis for right standing. It is Christ alone who saves, by grace alone, through faith alone. Christ is the basis of salvation; grace is its motive; faith is its instrument. We must resist the tendency to view faith as the basis of our justification rather than Christ's righteousness.

But Won't Such Teaching Inhibit Holiness?

One of the most remarkable ironies of church history is that those periods especially marked by a fear of emphasizing the objective, free, sovereign, and utterly gracious character of salvation are also among the most ungodly ages. The moralism of Pelagius may have seen Augustinianism as a perfidious rejection of Christ's moral instruction, but Pelagianism has failed to produce godliness in any generation. As if it were not enough that it is under the divine anathema for proclaiming another gospel—which is no gospel—this naturalistic and moralistic religion never even achieves its intended results, "having a form of godliness but denying its power" (2 Timothy 3:5). For the power of godliness is the same as the power of God unto salvation: the gospel of free justification by the imputation of an alien righteousness (Romans 1:16).

Many "testimonies" one hears for becoming a Christian these days could be given by Mormons, or others whose lifestyles have been greatly improved; but where is the gospel? The good news is not what happens *inside* of me, but what happened two thousand years ago *for* me! It is the testimony of eyewitnesses to *that* event that really matters, if we are gospel-centered people. Although modern evangelicalism focuses its outreach on the testimony of "changed lives" instead of the life, death, and resurrection of the God-man for us, there seems to be a dearth of changed lives. We have lost the power of godliness because we have set aside the power of God unto salvation. By turning from the gospel to more "practical" approaches, we have not only failed to honor the gospel, but have undermined the only possibility of genuine conversion and growth in holiness.

In our day, the doctrine of justification is hardly known—a casualty of the growing religious ignorance of our age. But it is more than that. Whenever the church forgets anything at all, she forgets this: that God has spared her not because of *her* goodness, but because of *His* (Deuteronomy 9:1–6). As therapeutic and managerial categories threaten to wash biblical categories of sin and grace out to sea, we are watching the tendency of the human heart at work. We all want a manageable, affable, user-friendly deity, and that has been true ever since the Fall. Sure, we all make mistakes, but if we only have enough good examples to imitate and practical instructions to follow, surely we would shape up! Recovery, not redemption, is the felt need of the hour.

In my own life, as well as my pastoral ministry, the practical importance of getting these truths down into our hearts has been proven again and again. For one thing, we are still sinners, regardless of how long we have been believers. "Simultaneously justified and sinful" is the condition in which the believer finds himself through all his days until sanctification lurches joyfully into perfect conformity to God's holy will in the heavenly Promised Land.

As the Heidelberg Catechism puts it: "Even the very best we do in this life is imperfect and stained with sin" (Q. 62). But this perspective is on the way out in many Christian circles, due to a strange combination of mystical anti-nomianism and perfectionism (especially from lingering "Higher Life" influences).

Baptist seminary professor E. Glenn Hinson warns of "an imperialism of Pauline theology" in classical Reformation teaching. The problem with those who defend this perspective is that they "still adhere to the juridical understanding of Luther" and ignore "the traditional Catholic view that justification also involves the transformation of the sinner." The danger of this "Reformation" view is that it takes "a narrow view of grace, seeing it as something given rather than as the living God invading our lives and transforming us."[1] Similarly, Fuller Seminary professor Russell P. Spittler wonders: "But can it really be true—saint and sinner simultaneously? I wish it were so . . . I hope it's true! I simply fear it's not."[2] Asbury Seminary professor Laurence W. Wood adds that "justification is freedom from the acts of sin," "an infusion of divine love." "Consequently," he argues, "*in the end* we will be justified if through faith and obedience we have so conducted our life."[3]

What we are finding again and again within mainstream evangelical circles is the growing acceptance of views that, at their best, are revivals of the errors of Rome and, at their worst, represent explicitly Pelagian notions. The quotation from Professor Wood above was a sobering example of the former. Examples of the latter may be found especially in Clark Pinnock and his associates, now working on the project of eliminating the vestiges not only of classical Protestant theology, but of Augustinianism altogether.[4]

But this is happening at the academic level. Most Christians today, like medieval laypeople, are simply left in ignorance, while sermons on self-esteem, stress, and success deepen the narcissism of the "me generation." Eighty-four percent of professing evangelicals claim that in salvation "God helps those who help themselves," which makes sense when one learns that seventy-seven percent believe that human beings are basically good. Whatever the explicit revisions in evangelical theology that may be called for in the seminaries, it seems that the diet in popular preaching, evangelism, worship, discipleship, publishing, and broadcasting favors this "megashift." If Pelagianism is the religion of the natural man, as B. B. Warfield insisted, it should come as no surprise that this is becoming the unofficial creed of a creedless and unthinking church.

But what about us? How are we executing our duties, we who regard ourselves as heirs of the Apostles, Augustine, the Reformers, and the Puritans? That justification is useful for being set right with God in the first place is granted. But too often we stop there, moving on to other doctrines to drive the Christian life. To be sure, we are commissioned to preach the whole counsel of God, and there can be no genuine growth in Christ unless we understand the new birth, sanctification, union with Christ, ministry of Word and sacrament, and the practical duties. It is not just some of the doctrines of salvation, but all of them that must be recovered before genuine awakening can take place and produce, by the Holy Spirit's power, men and women who are growing up into mature discipleship. Nevertheless, justification must not only be at the heart of our understanding of how we are initially accepted by God, but must never be moved to the periphery in any discussion of the Christian life.

In many cases I have heard people say that there was grace for them when they first became Christians, but now they are not quite sure. God *saved* me as a sinner, but does he still save me *as a sinner*? Especially in "victorious Christian life" schemes, where indwelling sin is downplayed in favor of a type of mystical perfectionism, many come to believe (implicitly at least) that they were justified by grace alone through faith alone at first, but now they are not quite sure. So they go back to the clothing racks of fig leaves and cobwebs.

If "the very best we do in this life is imperfect and stained with sin," can we ever switch our reliance on God's favor from justification to sanctification? While our growth in godliness often provides precious tokens of God's persevering grace in our lives, will it ever be sufficient in this life to anchor our confidence? "For since no perfection can come to us" in this life, says Calvin, "and the law moreover announces death and judgment to all who do not maintain perfect righteousness in works, it will always have grounds for accusing and condemning us unless, on the contrary, God's mercy counters it, and by continual forgiveness of sins repeatedly acquits us."[5]

A Distinction We Can't Live (or Grow) Without

Here once more we are assisted by the biblical categories recovered by the Reformers and Puritans. At the heart of the Reformation's hermeneutics was the distinction between law and gospel. For the Reformers, this was not equivalent to Old Testament and New Testament, respectively; rather, it meant that, in the words of Theodore Beza, "We divide this Word into two principal parts or kinds: the one is called the law, the other the gospel. For all the rest can be gathered under the one or other of these two headings." The law "is written by nature in our hearts," while "What we call the gospel (good news) is a doctrine which is not at all in us by nature, but which is revealed from Heaven (Matthew 16:17; John 1:13)." The Law leads us to Christ in the Gospel by condemning us and causing us to despair of our own "righteousness." "Ignorance of this distinction between law and gospel," Beza wrote, "is one of the principal sources of the abuses which corrupted and still corrupt Christianity."[6]

Luther made this hermeneutic central, but both traditions of the Protestant Reformation jointly affirm this key distinction. In much of medieval preaching, the law and gospel were so confused that the "good news" seemed to be that Jesus was a "kinder, gentler Moses," who softened the law into easier exhortations, such as loving God and neighbor from the heart. The Reformers saw Rome as teaching that the Gospel was simply an easier "law" than that of the Old Testament. Instead of following a lot of rules, God expects only love and heart-felt surrender. Calvin replied, "As if we could think of anything more difficult than to love God with all our heart, all our soul, and all our strength! Compared with this law, everything could be considered easy. . . . [For] the law cannot do anything else than to accuse and blame all to a man, to convict, and, as it were, apprehend them; in fine, to condemn them in God's judgment: that God alone may justify, that all flesh may keep silence before him."[7] Thus, Calvin observes, Rome could only see the gospel as that which enables believers to become righteous by obedience and that which is "a compensation for their lack," not realizing that the law requires perfection, not approximation.[8]

Of course, no one claims to have arrived at perfection, and yet, Calvin says, many do claim "to have yielded completely to God, [claiming that] they have kept the law in part and are, in respect to this part, righteous."9 Only the terror of the law can shake us of this self-confidence. Thus, the law condemns and drives us to Christ so that the gospel can comfort without any threats or exhortations that might lead to doubt. In one of his earliest writings, Calvin defended this evangelical distinction between law and gospel:

> All this will readily be understood by describing the Law and describing the Gospel and then comparing them. Therefore, the Gospel is the message, the salvation-bringing proclamation concerning Christ that he was sent by God the Father . . . to procure eternal life. The Law is contained in precepts; it threatens, it burdens, it promises no good will. The Gospel acts without threats; it does not drive one on by precepts, but rather teaches us about the supreme good will of God towards us. Let whoever therefore is desirous of having a plain and honest understanding of the Gospel, test everything by the above descriptions of the Law and

> the Gospel. Those who do not follow this
> method of treatment will never be ade-
> quately versed in the Philosophy of
> Christ.[10]

While the law continues to guide the believer
in the Christian life, Calvin insists that it can
never be confused with the good news. Even *after* conversion, the believer is in desperate need
of the gospel because he reads the commands,
exhortations, threats, and warnings of the law,
and often wavers in his certain confidence because he does not see in himself this righteousness that is required. Am I *really* surrendered?
Have I *truly* yielded in every area of my life?
What if I have not experienced the same things
that other Christians regard as normative? Do I
really possess the Holy Spirit? What if I fall
into serious sin? These are questions that we all
face in pastoral ministry as well as in our own
lives. What will restore our peace and hope in
the face of such questions? The Reformers, with
the prophets and apostles, were convinced that
only the gospel could bring such comfort to the
struggling Christian.

Without this constant emphasis in preaching, one can never truly worship nor serve God

in liberty; his gaze will be fastened on himself in either despair or self-righteousness rather than on Christ. Law and gospel must both ever be preached, both for conviction and instruction; but the conscience will never rest, Calvin says, so long as Gospel is mixed with Law. "Consequently, this Gospel does not impose any commands, but rather reveals God's goodness, His mercy and His benefits."[11] This distinction, Calvin says with Luther and the other Reformers, marks the difference between Christianity and paganism: "All who deny this turn the whole of the Gospel upside down; they utterly bury Christ, and destroy all true worship of God."[12]

Ursinus, primary author of the Heidelberg Catechism, said that the law-gospel distinction has "comprehended the sum and substance of the sacred Scriptures," and that it constitutes "the chief and general divisions of the holy scriptures, and comprises the entire doctrine comprehended therein."[13]

To confuse law and gospel is to corrupt the faith at its core.[14] While the law must be preached as divine instruction for the Christian life, it must never be used to shake believers from the confidence that Christ is their "righteousness, holiness and redemption" (1 Corinthians 1:30). The believer goes to the law, and loves that law for its divine wisdom, for it reveals the will of the One to whom we are now reconciled by the gospel. But the believer cannot find pardon, mercy, victory, or even the power to obey it by going to the law itself any more *after* his conversion than before. It is still always the law that commands and the gospel that gives. This is why every sermon must be carefully crafted on this foundational distinction.

As he watched the Baptist Church in England give way to moralism in the so-called "Downgrade Controversy," Charles Spurgeon declared, "There is no point on which men make greater mistakes than on the relation which exists between the law and the gospel. Some men put the law instead of the gospel; others put gospel instead of the law. A certain class maintains that the law and the gospel are mixed. . . . These men understand not the truth and are false teachers."[15]

In our day, these categories are once again confused in even the most conservative churches. Even where the categories of psychology, marketing, and politics do not replace those of law and gospel, much of evangelical preaching today softens the law and confuses the gospel with exhortations, often leaving people with the impression that God does not expect the perfect righteousness prescribed in the law, but a generally good heart and attitude and avoidance of major sins. In spite of general affirmations of gospel doctrines, a gentle moralism prevails in much of evangelical preaching today, and one rarely hears the law preached as God's condemnation and wrath, but as helpful suggestions for a more fulfilled life.

Sometimes this error is due less to conviction than to a lack of precision. For instance, we often hear calls to "live the gospel," yet nowhere in Scripture are we called to "live the gospel." Instead, we are told to *believe* the gospel and *obey* the law, receiving God's favor from the one and God's guidance from the other. The gospel—or good news—is not that God will help us achieve His favor with His help, but that someone else lived the law in our place and fulfilled all righteousness.

Others confuse the law and gospel by replacing the demands of the law with the simple command to "surrender all" or "make

Jesus Lord and Savior," as if this one little work secured eternal life. J. Gresham Machen, earlier this century, declared, "According to modern liberalism, faith is essentially the same as 'making Christ master' of one's life. . . . But that simply means that salvation is thought to be obtained by our obedience to the commands of Christ. Such teaching is just a sublimated form of legalism."[16] In another work, Machen added:

> What good does it do to me to tell me that the type of religion presented in the Bible is a very fine type of religion and that the thing for me to do is just to start practicing that type of religion now? . . . I will tell you, my friend. It does me not one tiniest little bit of good. . . . What I need first of all is not exhortation, but a gospel, not directions for saving myself but knowledge of how God has saved me. Have you any good news? That is the question that I ask of you. I know your exhortations will not help me. But if anything has been done to save me, will you not tell me the facts?[17]

Does that mean that the Word of God does not command our obedience, or that such obedience is optional? Certainly not! But it does mean that obedience must not be confused with the gospel. Our best obedience is corrupted, so how could *that* be good news? The gospel is that Christ was crucified for our sins and was raised for our justification. The gospel *produces* new life, new experiences, and a new obedience, but too often we confuse the fruit or effects with the gospel itself. Nothing that happens *within us* is, properly speaking, "gospel," but it is the gospel's effect. Thus, Paul instructs us: "Only let your conduct be worthy of the gospel of Christ" (Philippians 1:27). While the gospel contains no commands or threats, the law indeed does; and the Christian is still obligated to both of these words he hears from the mouth of God. Like the Godhead or the two natures of Christ, we must neither divorce nor confuse Law and Gospel.

When the Law is softened into gentle promises and the Gospel is hardened into conditions and exhortations, the believer often finds himself in a deplorable state. As we have already seen, for those who know their own hearts, preaching that tries to tone down the Law by assuring them that God looks on the heart comes as bad news, not good news: "The heart is deceitful above all things" (Jeremiah 17:9). Many Christians have experienced the confusion of law and gospel in their diet, where the gospel was free and unconditional when they became believers, but was now pushed into the background to make room for an almost exclusive emphasis on exhortations. Again, it is not that exhortations do not have their place, but they must never be confused with the gospel; and that gospel of divine forgiveness is as important for sinful believers to hear as it is for unbelievers. Nor can we assume that believers ever progress beyond the stage where they need to hear the gospel, as if the good news ended at conversion. For, as Calvin said, "We are all partly unbelievers throughout our lives." We must constantly hear God's promise in order to counter the doubts and fears that are natural to us.

But there are many, especially in our narcissistic age, whose ignorance of the law leads them into a carnal security. Thus, people often conclude that they are "safe and secure from all alarm" because they walked an aisle, prayed a prayer, or signed a card, even though they have never had to give up their own fig leaves in order to be clothed with the righteousness of the Lamb of God. Or perhaps, although they have not perfectly loved God and neighbor, they

conclude that they are at least "yielded," "surrendered," or "letting the Spirit have His way";
or, still more boldly, that they are "living in
victory over all known sin" and enjoying the
"higher life." Deluding themselves and others,
they need to be stripped of their fig leaves in
order to be clothed with the skins of the Lamb
of God. Thus, Machen writes:

> A new and more powerful proclamation of
> law is perhaps the most pressing need of
> the hour; men would have little difficulty
> with the gospel if they had only learned
> the lesson of the law. As it is, they are
> turning aside from the Christian pathway;
> they are turning to the village of Morality,
> and to the house of Mr. Legality, who is
> reported to be very skillful in relieving
> men of their burdens. . . . 'Making Christ
> Master' in the life, putting into practice 'the
> principles of Christ' by one's own efforts
> —these are merely new ways of earning
> salvation by one's obedience to God's
> commands. And they are undertaken be-
> cause of a lax view of what those com-
> mands are. So it always is: a low view of
> law always brings legalism in religion; a
> high view of law makes a man a seeker af-
> ter grace.[18]

The irony of the Christian life is that the driving force behind our sanctification is the very opposite of what human nature would suggest. Natural religion insists that we must be moved to good works by fear of punishment or the hope of rewards, while biblical faith declares that it is the announcement of justification by grace alone, apart from works, that leads to good works. What could be more obviously false to human wisdom? Surely an obsession with "grace alone" will lead to presumption and license, we reason. And, to be sure, unregenerate professing Christians will exploit the gospel for this very purpose (Jude 4). Nevertheless, legalists and antinomians both follow the assumptions of natural reason in this matter: both believe that grace leads to license because neither has truly learned the power of godliness, which is the gospel.

John Murray wisely writes that the law not only cannot provide justification: "Law can do nothing to relieve the bondage of sin; it accentuates and confirms that bondage," so that "there is an absolute antithesis between the potency and provisions of law and the potency and provisions of grace."[19]

Another helpful way of making this point is

to follow the distinction between the indicative and imperative moods. The indicative tells us what is already true of us, while the imperative refers to the obligations we have in the light of that reality. In most cases, the shift from indicative to imperative moods is announced by the conjunction "therefore." In Romans 6, for instance, we are told that we are buried with Christ in baptism and raised with Him to new life. Everything in the first half of chapter 6 is in the indicative mood. We are not commanded to die, to "let go and let God," to "surrender all on the altar," or to achieve victory. We are simply told that God has already buried us with Christ and raised us in newness of life. He has given us a new heart and has placed His Spirit within us, fulfilling the prophetic expectations. Then, in the second half of chapter 6, we are told to present our bodies to God in holy service. The imperative follows the indicative rather than leading to it.

Lest our confidence in this newness of life that has already been secured for us lead us again to self-confidence or triumphalism, Paul moves on in Romans 7 to describe the reality of indwelling sin and the constant struggle that *is* sanctification. In Scripture, it is not the absence of war with sin, but the presence of war with sin, that becomes the characteristic mark and evidence of sanctification. When people conclude that they are probably not truly converted because they still struggle with indwelling sin, they are actually confirming their calling! It is not the unregenerate who struggle with their sinfulness (1 Corinthians 2:14), but believers, as Paul observes. He loves God's law and submits himself to its counsel, but he finds another factor at work in his life: indwelling sin. It is this battle that guarantees a progressive rather than immediate sanctification. Although Paul expresses deep dissatisfaction with his sanctification, his soul is restored once more when he lifts his gaze from himself to Christ (Romans 7:24–25).

Thus, the whole of our Christian life is a constant process of realizing God's judgment and justification, moving from self-loathing to fixing "our eyes on Jesus, the author and perfecter of our faith" (Hebrews 12:2). It is a process of constantly being stripped of our fig leaves to be clothed with Christ. Joyfully accepting the new heart and the new life that are ours in Christ by the power of the abiding Spirit, we fight earnestly against indwelling sin, never despairing in spite of our failures and weaknesses because our Captain has already won the war to end all wars. Let us then fight on!

---

[1] Donald L. Alexander, ed., *Christian Spirituality: Five Views of Sacntification* (Downers Grove: InterVarsity Press, 1988), pp. 44–46.

[2] Ibid., pp. 42-43

[3] Ibid., pp. 37–38

[4] Clark Pinnock, ed., *The Grace of God and the Will of Man* (Grand Rapids, Mich.: Zondervan, 1989).

[5] John Calvin, *Institutes of the Christian Religion*, 3.14.10.

[6] Theodore Beza, *The Christian Faith*, trans. James Clark (East Sussex, England: Focus Christian Ministries Trust, 1992), pp. 40–41. Published first at Geneva in 1558 as the *Confession de foi du chrétien*.

[7] Calvin, *Institutes* (1536 edition), 2.7.5; trans. by F. L. Battles (Grand Rapids: Eerdmans, 1975), pp. 30-1; cf. the 1559 edition, 2.11.10.

[8] Calvin, *Institutes* (1559 edition), 3.14.13.

[9] Ibid.

[10] These words were delivered by Nicolas Cop on his assumption of the rectorship of the University of Paris; there is a wide (though not undisputed) consensus among Calvin scholars that Calvin was the author. They are quoted in F. L. Battle's translation of the 1536 edition of the *Institutes* (Grand Rapids, Mich.: Eerdmans, 1975), p. 365.

[11] Ibid., p. 366.

[12] Ibid., p. 369.

[13] Ursinus, *Commentary on the Heidelberg Catechism*(Phillipsburg, NJ: Presbyterian and Reformed, from 2nd American ed., 1852), p. 2.

[14] Ibid., p. 3.

[15] Charles Spurgeon, *New Park Street Pulpit* (Pasadena, Tex.: Pilgrim Publications, 1975), vol. 1, p. 285.

[16] J. Gresham Machen, *Christianity and Liberalism* (New York: Macmillan, 1923), p. 143.

[17] J. Gresham Machen, *Christian Faith in the Modern World* (New York: Macmillan, 1936), p. 57.

[18] J. Gresham Machen, *What is Faith?* (New York: Macmillan, 1925), pp. 137, 139, 152.

[19] John Murray, *The New International Commentary on the New Testament: Romans* (Grand Rapids, Mich.: Eerdmans, 1968), p. 229.

Obedience: Love or Legalism?

John MacArthur

A few years ago I wrote a book that became the subject of widespread controversy. That book, *The Gospel According to Jesus*, argued that Jesus is presented in the gospel as both Savior *and* Lord, and He demands obedience. To be precise, Jesus is actually *never* presented as "Savior and Lord" in the Bible; it is *always* as "Lord and Savior." Therefore, those who remain obstinately unwilling to obey Him are actually guilty of rejecting the Christ who is offered in the gospel. So the person who claims to accept Jesus as Savior while persisting to refuse His lordship has actually spurned the true Christ and therefore is no Christian.

That, of course, is nothing more or less than what mainstream evangelicalism has historically affirmed. Virtually all the important Protestant statements of faith say exactly the same thing. In the Westminster Shorter Catechism, for example, Question 86 asks, "What is faith in Jesus Christ?" The answer: "Faith in

Jesus Christ is a saving grace, whereby we receive and rest upon Him alone for salvation, *as He is offered to us in the gospel*" (emphasis added). Question 87 goes on to define repentance unto life as "a saving grace, whereby a sinner, out of a true sense of his sin, and apprehension of the mercy of God in Christ, doth, with grief and hatred of his sin, turn from it unto God, *with full purpose of, and endeavor after, new obedience*" (emphasis added).

Our obedience does not *merit* salvation, of course. But genuine conversion to Christ inevitably produces obedience. Therefore, while obedience is never a *condition* for salvation, it is nonetheless always salvation's *fruit*. That is why Scripture speaks of obedience as an essential evidence of true Christianity: "He that saith, I know Him, and keepeth not His commandments, is a liar, and the truth is not in him" (1 John 2:4). "In this the children of God are manifest, and the children of the devil: whosoever doeth not righteousness is not of God" (3:10). "He that doeth good is of God: but he that doeth evil hath not seen God" (3 John 11).

Do We Obey out of Love or out of Duty?

In the midst of the controversy over these things, a fellow pastor wrote me:

Dear John,

I am sympathetic to your stance on the lordship of Christ. You are quite right in teaching that the gospel calls sinners to repentance and calls for their obedience to Christ as Lord. His lordship is as crucial to the gospel message as His deity. In fact, as you point out, His deity and His lordship are so inextricably bound together that a Christ who is not Lord of all is not the Christ who saves. The modern notion that the sinner can reject Christ as Lord but receive Him as Savior is foreign to all the historic creeds. To my way of thinking, any message that excludes the lordship of Christ is not the gospel at all.

If you don't mind, however, I would like to offer a criticism that I hope you will find helpful, not hurtful: I notice that you present Christian obedience as a *duty*. You often cite the biblical passages that speak of the Christian as a bondservant, as if this meant we are abject slaves to Him. Your stress is on the Lord's authority to command obedience. And therefore you speak of obedience as an *obligation* to which the believer is bound.

I see a different emphasis in Scripture. Faith works through love (Galatians 5:6). The Christian obeys Christ out of sheer love for Him. Obedience for the Christian is not so much a duty as it is a delight. Believers obey because that is where they

find their satisfaction, *not* because they are
bound to do so. We obey out of love for
Christ, not out of fear, and not out of duty.
I believe this perspective is essential to
joyous Christian living. It is the whole
difference between legalism and true
Christianity.

I sincerely appreciated that man's comments. And I agree that it is possible to place so
much stress on the *duty* of obedience that we
lose sight of the *joy* of it. After all, the Christian's obedience should be a delight. Love for
Christ is a higher motive than fear. So there is
certainly some sound truth in what this man
wrote.

Nonetheless, the danger of overemphasis is
very real on both sides of this truth. It is not
quite right to say "We obey out of love for
Christ . . . and *not* out of duty." Duty and love
are not incompatible motives. A father provides
for his children because he loves them. Yet it is
also his legal and moral duty to do so. The fact
that a man loves his children does not lessen
his duty to them. The more he loves them, the
more he will see the duty as a joy and not a
drudgery. But even when the duty is a delight,
it should not diminish the father's solemn
sense of duty.

Our obedience to Christ is like that. Certainly we ought to obey Him out of a deep love for Him. And the sheer joy of pleasing Him should permeate our obedience. Yet we should never think of obedience as anything less than a sacred duty. Our love for Christ does not make submission to Him elective. Christ is still our Master, and our relationship with Him carries a great weight of responsibility. We ought to serve Him as loving, devoted bondservants. "Abject slaves" is probably not too strong a term.

Jesus Himself underscored this very thing:

> But which of you, having a servant plowing or feeding cattle, will say unto him by and by, when he is come from the field, Go and sit down to meat? And will not rather say unto him, Make ready wherewith I may sup, and gird thyself, and serve me, till I have eaten and drunken; and afterward thou shalt eat and drink? Doth he thank that servant because he did the things that were commanded him? I trow not. So likewise ye, when ye shall have done all those things which are commanded you, say, We are unprofitable servants; we have done that which was our duty to do (Luke 17:7–10).

That imagery paints a clear picture of the kind of servitude we are expected to render to Christ as His servants.

But that's only half the picture. Our Lord also called for the obedience of love: "If ye love Me, keep My commandments" (John 14:15). And He elevated those who obey to the level of *friends*:

> Ye are My friends, if ye do whatsoever I command you. Henceforth I call you not servants; for the servant knoweth not what his lord doeth: but I have called you friends; for all things that I have heard of My Father I have made known unto you (John 15:14–15).

Obviously, our Lord viewed our love for Him and our duty to Him as motives for obedience that are inextricably and necessarily bound together: "He that hath My commandments, and keepeth them, he it is that loveth Me" (John 14:21). "If ye keep My commandments, ye shall abide in My love; even as I have kept My Father's commandments, and abide in His love" (John 15:10).

Far from being a drudgery, Christian obedience is thus the bond of our relationship with Christ and the source of our deepest joy. And the fact that we are obliged to submit to His lordship should never alter the joy we find in doing so.

Of course, because we are still fleshly creatures, our obedience is not *always* joyful. And so we must realize that even when our hearts are not brimming with the joy of the Lord, obedience remains our duty. We are to obey when it brings us pleasure, but we also must obey even when we do not feel like it. *Both* our love for the Lord and our sense of duty to Him should motivate this obedience. One must never cancel out the other.

I fear that the church in our generation is losing sight of the role of duty in the Christian life. Multitudes see "duty" as something altogether foreign to Christianity. Compliance with the commandments of Christ is deemed optional. If you dare suggest that obedience is mandatory, you will be branded a legalist.

"We are not under the law, but under grace" has become the mantra of modern Christianity. But most who chant that phrase today mean something dramatically different from what the apostle Paul meant in Romans 6:14 when he wrote, "Ye are not under the law, but under grace."

In What Sense Are We Freed from the Law Under Grace?

The phrase "under the law" occurs at least ten times in Paul's epistles, so we know it is a crucial concept in his theology. In Galatians 3:23, for example, He writes, "Before faith came, we were kept *under the law*." Now, however, he says as Christians we are "*not* under the law" (Galatians 5:18).

I often hear Christians recite the phrase "not under the law, but under grace" as if it meant no standard of law whatsoever is ever binding on believers. Grace is seen as a grand permissiveness, contrasting with the uncompromising moral standard of the law. One man wrote,

> According to Paul, I am not under law. That has radical practical consequences for my Christian life. It means I do not have to look over my shoulder at the law and judge my life by it. The law was a negative standard. It was filled with prohibitions and punishments. Grace is the opposite. It is filled with positive inducements and promises. Which would you rather have as a rule of life? *I* live under grace, not law. And that means whenever the law brings its negative message—*when it says, "thou shalt not"*—it does not apply to me.

The notion that no law is binding on the Christian is a classic form of *antinomianism*. This type of thinking sets grace *against* law, as if the two were antithetical. It has some dire theological consequences.

It is crucial to understand that in terms of moral standards, grace does not permit what the law prohibits. Grace never signifies the lowering of God's moral demands. The word "grace" in Scripture signifies a lot of things, but licentiousness is not one of them. In fact, those who turn the grace of God into promiscuity are expressly condemned as false teachers (Jude 4).

Grace, according to Scripture, is the undeserved kindness of a sovereign God. More than that, grace means that God mercifully gives us the very opposite of what our sin merits. Grace includes not merely pardon for our sin, but also the power to live a transformed life. In other words, the grace Scripture describes is a dynamic force, the sovereign influence of a holy God operating in the lives of undeserving sinners. This is the key to grace: it is God working in us to secure our working for Him (Philippians 2:13). Grace first transforms the heart and thus makes the believer wholly willing to trust and obey. Grace then conveys upon us both the desire and the strength to fulfill God's good pleasure. Far more than mere pardon, grace also insures our obedience, gives us a true love for God, and transforms our lives in every sense.

Ultimately, grace totally conforms us to the image of Christ (Romans 8:29). Even now, grace is doing what the law could not do: it is fulfilling the righteous requirement of the law in us (Romans 8:3–4).

So the moral standard set by the law does not change under grace. Indeed, it could not; it is a reflection of God's character. But divine grace actually empowers us to fulfill the moral demands of the law in a way that the law alone could never do.

Just what *does* the apostle Paul mean when he says we are not under law? There are two ways in which Scripture clearly teaches we are not under law:

1. We are not under the ceremonial law.

Paul's epistle to the Galatians uses the expression "under the law" several times (3:23; 4:4–5, 21; 5:18). Paul wrote this epistle to confront the influence of the Judaizers, Jewish legalists who were trying to impose the ceremonies and rituals of the Mosaic law on all Christians. According to the Judaizers, in order to become a true Christian, a Gentile first had to become a Jewish proselyte.

Circumcision and the dietary laws became the test issues. This had been a running dispute in the early church from the very beginning. The earliest church council in Jerusalem had been convened to deal with this very question. According to Acts 15:5, some Pharisees who had converted to Christianity rose up and demanded that Gentiles who joined the church be circumcised and directed to obey the law of Moses. Luke records what happened:

> And the apostles and elders came together for to consider of this matter. And when there had been much disputing, Peter rose up, and said unto them, Men and brethren, ye know how that a good while ago God made choice among us, that the Gentiles by my mouth should hear the word of the gospel, and believe. And God, which knoweth the hearts, bare them witness, giving them the Holy Ghost, even as He did unto us; and put no difference between us and them, purifying their hearts by faith. Now therefore why tempt ye God, to put a yoke upon the neck of the disciples, which neither our fathers nor we were able to bear? But we believe that through the grace of the Lord Jesus Christ we shall be saved, even as they (Acts 15:6–11).

The council saw a heated debate on the question. But, led by James, they ultimately came to consensus:

> Trouble not them, which from among the
> Gentiles are turned to God: but . . . write
> unto them, that they abstain from pollu-
> tions of idols, and from fornication, and
> from things strangled, and from blood
> (verses 19–20).

This meant that the ceremonial requirements of the Mosaic law were not to be imposed upon the church. Circumcision could not be required of the Gentiles. Strict adherence to the dietary laws was not to be prescribed. But in order not to offend the Jewish brethren, the Gentiles were asked to abstain from the most offensive dietary practices: the eating of meat offered to idols, of strangled animals, and of blood. Even those restrictions were not imposed as binding matters of legal necessity, but were required of the Gentiles only as a matter of charity toward their Jewish brethren.

How do we know that these prohibitions against eating certain things were not meant to be a permanent standard for the church for all time? As Paul wrote to Timothy, nothing is to be viewed as ceremonially unclean if it is re-

ceived with thanksgiving (1 Timothy 4:4). But
these measures were called for by the Jerusalem
Council in the primitive church as a matter of
charity to the many Jewish believers who saw
such practices as inherently pagan. The apostle
Paul summed up this principle of freedom and
deference in Romans 14:14–15:

> I know, and am persuaded by the Lord
> Jesus, that there is nothing unclean of it-
> self: but to him that esteemeth any thing
> to be unclean, to him it is unclean. But if
> thy brother be grieved with thy meat,
> now walkest thou not charitably.

A side note is necessary here with regard to
the restriction against "fornication." The biblical prohibitions against fornication are moral,
not ceremonial, commandments. So why was it
necessary to include a ban on fornication in the
Jerusalem Council's instructions? After all,
fornication would clearly be deemed morally
reprehensible and strictly forbidden under *any*
standard in the early church. And from the
beginning the dispute that prompted the Jerusalem Council had to do only with the ceremonial aspects of Moses' law.

The answer lies in an understanding of the
pagan religions from which many of these

Gentile converts had come. The practice of ceremonial fornication was common. Many of the pagan shrines featured temple prostitutes, with whom acts of fornication were deemed religious experiences. So when it forbade "pollutions of idols, and . . . fornication," the Council was prohibiting the observance of pagan religious ceremonies. And when it called for abstinence "from things strangled, and from blood," it was asking the Gentiles to have respect for the deeply ingrained scruples of their Jewish brethren, which resulted from lifelong obedience to Mosaic ceremonies.

In other words, pagan religious ceremonies were forbidden, and Jewish ceremonies were not made the standard. But charity was enjoined upon all.

It is crucial to see that this Council was explicitly *not* establishing the Mosaic ceremonial law *or any portion of it* as the standard for the church. The New Testament is explicit throughout that the types and ceremonies of the Law are *not* binding on Christians. The dietary and ceremonial requirements of Moses' law "are a shadow of things to come; but the body is of Christ" (Colossians 2:17). The priesthood and temple worship of the Old Testament economy also "serve unto the example and shadow of heavenly things" (Hebrews 8:5). Christ is the fulfillment of all those observances, and He is the Mediator of a new covenant. To cling to the types and shadows of the old covenant is in effect to deny that Christ, the One foreshadowed, is superior. Therefore, the ceremonial aspects of Moses' law have no place whatsoever in the Church.

Why did both Paul and the writer of Hebrews view the Judaizers' doctrine as such a serious error? Because by retreating to the types and shadows of the old covenant, these people were guilty of replacing the all-important reality of a living Savior with outmoded symbols that only *pointed* to Him. Their attachment to those now-barren religious emblems *necessarily* thrust them into a system of works. To return to the old covenant was a *de facto* rejection of Christ in favor of obsolete types and symbols.

In one of the most unusual encounters between two apostles recorded anywhere in Scripture, Peter and Paul had a very public conflict over the question of obedience to the ceremonial law. Paul describes the confrontation in Galatians 2:11–14:

> When Peter was come to Antioch, I withstood him to the face, because he was

> to be blamed. For before that certain came
> from James, he did eat with the Gentiles:
> but when they were come, he withdrew
> and separated himself, fearing them which
> were of the circumcision. And the other
> Jews dissembled likewise with him; in-
> somuch that Barnabas also was carried
> away with their dissimulation. But when
> I saw that they walked not uprightly ac-
> cording to the truth of the gospel, I said
> unto Peter before them all, If thou, being a
> Jew, livest after the manner of Gentiles,
> and not as do the Jews, why compellest
> thou the Gentiles to live as do the Jews?

The issue at stake here was no longer the
question of charity toward Jewish brethren, but
the whole doctrine of justification by faith.
Apparently, even after the Jerusalem Council
had rendered its decision, the Judaizers nevertheless reverted to demanding circumcision for
every Gentile convert. They were actually suggesting that observance of the ceremonial law
was essential for justification. And, as Paul suggests, Peter, of all people, should have known
better: "Knowing that a man is not justified by
the works of the law, but by the faith of Jesus
Christ, even we have believed in Jesus Christ,
that we might be justified by the faith of Christ,
and not by the works of the law: for by the

works of the law shall no flesh be justified" (verse 16).

2. We are not under the law for justification.

The centerpiece of New Testament theology is justification by faith. This is the doctrine that makes Christianity distinct. Every other religion in the world teaches some system of human merit. Christianity alone teaches that the merit necessary for our salvation is supplied by God on our behalf.

Justification is defined theologically as that act of God whereby He declares the believing sinner righteous.

When God justifies a sinner, he looks at the person and says, "I accept that person as completely righteous." It is a divine "not guilty" verdict, and more. It elevates the sinner from the condemnation he deserves to a position of divine privilege in Christ.

Justification poses a huge theological problem. Proverbs 17:15 says, "He that justifieth the wicked, and he that condemneth the just, even they both are abomination to the Lord." In other words, God Himself strictly forbids us to declare a guilty person righteous. And God says definitively in Exodus 23:7, "I will not justify the wicked."

Two obstacles exist with regard to justifying

sinners. One is our sin. We accumulate guilt every time we sin, and true justice demands that every sin be punished. To let an evildoer go unpunished is by definition unjust. So God is obligated by His own perfect standard of justice to exact a full penalty for every sin.

The second obstacle to justification is our utter lack of merit. Not only do we accumulate guilt (or demerit) every time we sin, but we also lack the necessary merit. Even if our slate could be completely wiped clean, all we would have would be a blank slate. But in order to be acceptable to God, we are required to have the full merit that comes with perfect obedience to His law. Forgiveness for our sin isn't enough. We still need the merit of an absolutely perfect righteousness (Matthew 5:20, 48).

From the human perspective, those would seem to be impossible obstacles to the justification of any sinner. We can certainly understand the disciples' bewilderment when they saw these same difficulties: "Who then can be saved?" (Matthew 19:25).

However, there were people in Paul's day who thought that if they could just be as good as they could possibly be, they might earn enough merit to please God. This was the attitude behind the Judaizers' insistence on adhering to the ceremonial laws. They were trying to justify themselves before God through their own works.

They were trying to earn their own righteousness. That is the very definition of "self-righteous." Jesus' Sermon on the Mount was an attack on that kind of thinking. He pointed to the Pharisees, legalists who kept the law more fastidiously than anyone else. By human standards they were as "good" as it is possible to be. But Jesus said their goodness is simply not good enough to earn God's favor: "I say unto you that except your righteousness shall exceed the righteousness of the scribes and Pharisees, ye shall in no case enter into the kingdom of heaven" (Matthew 5:20).

Jesus was teaching as plainly as possible that God will be pleased with nothing but an absolutely perfect righteousness. He taught that it is not good enough to avoid killing; we must also avoid the sin of hatred (verse 22). He said if you lust in your heart, it is the same as committing adultery (verse 28). He set the standard as high as possible, and then said that if you don't attain that perfect standard of righteousness, you cannot enter the kingdom of heaven. And thus He condemned us all.

The apostle James destroyed any vestige of

hope we might have of being justified by law
when he wrote, "Whosoever shall keep the
whole law, and yet offend in one point, he is
guilty of all" (James 2:10).

What are we supposed to conclude? That we
cannot be justified by the works of the law. It is
utterly impossible. The apostle Paul under-
scores this same truth again and again:

> "Ye could not be justified by the law of
> Moses" (Acts 13:39).

> "What things soever the law saith, it saith
> to them who are under the law: that every
> mouth may be stopped, and all the world
> may become guilty before God. Therefore
> by the deeds of the law there shall no flesh
> be justified in his sight: for by the law is
> the knowledge of sin" (Romans 3:19–20).

> "The law worketh wrath" (Romans 4:15).

> "As many as are of the works of the law
> are under the curse: for it is written,
> Cursed is every one that continueth not in
> all things which are written in the book of
> the law to do them . . . No man is justified
> by the law in the sight of God" (Galatians
> 3:10–11).

Paul could not state it any more clearly than

that. To make the fatal mistake of thinking you can be justified by being good enough to make yourself acceptable to God is to put yourself under the condemnation of the law.

This was the heart of the problem in Galatia. People were teaching that it was necessary to obey the law *in order to be justified.* In chapter 1 Paul calls this "another gospel," and he pronounces a solemn curse on those who were teaching it.

When Paul spoke of those who were "under the law," he was speaking of people who thought they could be justified by obedience to the law. Two parallel expressions in Galatians make this extremely clear. One is Galatians 4:21: "Tell me, *ye that desire to be under the law,* do ye not hear the law?" (emphasis added). If they had listened to the law itself, they would have heard that it establishes impossible conditions for justification. It condemns those who fail to obey it. For sinners, the law could be a means of condemnation, but *never* a means of justification.

For a sinner to embrace the law as a means of justification is sheer folly. Yet there were those in Galatia who "desire[d] to be under the law" (4:21).

Notice the parallel expression in Galatians

5:4: "You who are seeking to be justified by law" (New American Standard Bible). Those who were seeking to be "justified by law" in Galatians 5:4 were the same as those who desired to be "under the law" in 4:21.

Therefore, to be "under the law" in Paul's terminology is to be *under the law as a means of justification.* It is crucial to understand how Paul uses this expression. When he says we are not under the law but under grace in Romans 6, he is not discarding the *moral teachings* of the law. He is not lending credence to any sort of antinomian doctrine. He is not minimizing the sin of disobedience to the moral teachings of the law. He is not disparaging the law itself. In fact, in Romans 7:12, he calls the law "holy, just, and good."

Paul's consistent teaching with regard to the law is that it can never be a means of justification. And when he says we are "not under law," he means we do not ground our justification in our own personal obedience.

We are no longer trying to justify ourselves by obedience to the law. We are justified by grace through faith, not by the works of the law (Galatians 2:16). And therefore we are no longer under the condemnation of the law.

How Can God Justify the Ungodly?

How, then, can we be justified? How can God declare guilty sinners righteous without lowering or compromising His own righteous standard?

The answer lies in the work of Christ on our behalf. In Galatians 4:4, the apostle states that Jesus Christ was born "under the law." Obviously, this does not mean merely that Jesus was born Jewish. It means that He was *under the law* in the Pauline sense, obligated to fulfill the law perfectly as a means of justification.

In this same context, in the span of two verses, Paul twice employs the phrase "under the law." There is a clear logical connection between the last phrase in verse 4 and the first phrase in verse 5: Christ was "made under the law, to redeem them that were under the law."

We've already said that the law cannot be a means of righteousness for sinners. But Christ was no sinner. He lived impeccably "under the law." Hebrews 4:15 tells us He "was in all points tempted like as we are, yet without sin." He fulfilled the law perfectly, to the letter. First Peter 2:22 says He "did no sin, neither was guile found in His mouth." Hebrews 7:26 says He is "holy, harmless, undefiled, separate from

sinners, and made higher than the heavens."
Thus His flawless obedience to the law earned
the perfect merit that is necessary to please
God.

If Christ was perfectly sinless, then He did
not deserve to die. As one "under the law," He
would have been subject to the curse of the law
if He had violated even one command, but of
course He did not—He *could* not, because He is
God. He fulfilled every aspect of the law to the
letter—to the jot and tittle.

Yet He did die. More than that, He suffered
the full wrath of God on the cross. Why?
Scripture tells us the guilt of our sin was imputed to Him, and Christ paid the price for it.
Consequently, the merit of His perfect obedience can be imputed to our account. That is the
meaning of 2 Corinthians 5:21: God "hath made
[Christ] to be sin for us, who knew no sin; that
we might be made the righteousness of God in
him."

His death takes care of our *guilt*, and His
perfect life supplies us with all the *merit* we
need to be acceptable to God. That is how God
overcame the two great obstacles to our justification. And as Paul says in Romans 3:26, that is
how God can remain just, and justify those
who believe in Jesus. Christ has personally paid

the penalty for their sin, and He has personally obtained a perfect righteousness on their behalf. So He can justify the ungodly (Romans 4:5).

Scripture teaches no other means of justification. This is at the core of all gospel truth. As early as Genesis 15:6, Scripture teaches that Abraham was justified by an imputed righteousness. Any time *any* sinner is redeemed in Scripture, it is by an imputed righteousness, not a righteousness that is somehow earned or achieved by the sinner for his own redemption.

Romans 4:6–7 says David also knew the blessedness of the man to whom God imputes righteousness apart from works. In fact, this is the whole point Paul is making in Romans 4: justification has always been by faith, not by works, and through a righteousness that is imputed to the believer. Abraham understood the doctrine of justification in that way. David knew the same truth. So from the beginning of Scripture to the end, we are taught that the only merit God accepts is a merit that is imputed to our account. He never pronounces us righteous because of our own works of righteousness.

On the contrary, God says all our righteousnesses are fatally flawed. They are of no more value to God than filthy rags (Isaiah

64:6). But that is how God sees our works—no matter how good they are by human standards. They are unacceptable, filthy, to God.

That is why *our* obedience can never be good enough. That is why those who hang their hope of heaven on their own good works only doom themselves.

How Deadly Is Legalism?

All of this should make it very clear that the legalism Paul condemned as "another gospel" is a brand of legalism that seeks to ground our justification in personal obedience rather than the imputed righteousness of Christ. How deadly is such legalism?

The apostle Paul suggested it was precisely what caused the majority of Israel to reject Christ: "They being ignorant of God's righteousness, and going about to establish their own righteousness, have not submitted themselves unto the righteousness of God" (Romans 10:3).

Turning aside from the perfect righteousness of Christ (which would have been imputed to them by faith), they opted instead for an imperfect righteousness of their own. They mistakenly assumed, like most people today, that the best they could do would be good enough for God.

Here is the good news of the gospel: for everyone who believes, Christ's blood counts as payment for all our sins, and His fulfillment of the law counts as all the merit we need. Romans 10:4 therefore says, "Christ is the end [Greek., *telos*, "the thing aimed at"] of the law for righteousness to every one that believeth." Christ is the fulfillment of everything the law intended. In Christ, the ultimate goal of the law, *a perfect righteousness*, is made available to every believer. His righteousness is imputed to us by faith, and that is why God accepts us in Christ and for Christ's sake.

To the apostle Paul himself, this truth had deeply personal implications. He had labored his whole life as a legalistic Pharisee trying to establish his own righteousness by the law. He described his efforts in Philippians 3:4–8:

> If any other man thinketh that he hath whereof he might trust in the flesh, I more: circumcised the eighth day, of the stock of Israel, of the tribe of Benjamin, a Hebrew of the Hebrews; as touching the law, a Pharisee; concerning zeal, persecuting the church; touching the righteousness which is in the law, blameless. But what things were gain to me, those I counted loss for Christ. Yea doubtless,

> and I count all things but loss for the ex-
> cellency of the knowledge of Christ Jesus
> my Lord: for whom I have suffered the
> loss of all things, and do count them but
> dung, that I may win Christ.

What was so important to Paul about dumping all his own righteousness? Why did he count a whole lifetime of good works as mere rubbish? Because he knew it was flawed. And he knew that in Christ he would be the recipient of a perfect righteousness. Notice verse 9: ". . . and be found in Him, not having mine own righteousness, which is of the law, but that which is through the faith of Christ, the righteousness which is of God by faith."

Any righteousness other than the imputed righteousness of Christ is mere legalism. It is incapable of saving anyone. More than that, it is an affront to God—as if we were to offer Him soiled rags and expect Him to applaud us for doing so. That kind of legalism is spiritually fatal.

How Is Christian Obedience Different from Legalism?

It has become fashionable in some circles to pin the label of "legalism" on any teaching that stresses obedience to Christ. At the beginning of this chapter I quoted someone who stated that "the whole difference between legalism and true Christianity" is sewn up in the issue of whether we view obedience as a duty.

Biblically, there is no basis for such thinking. The Christian is still obligated to obey God, even though we know our obedience in no sense provides grounds for our justification. That is precisely why our obedience should be motivated primarily by gratitude to and love for the Lord. We are free from the threat of eternal condemnation (Romans 8:1). We are free from the law of sin and death (verse 2), and empowered by God's grace both to will and to do of His good pleasure (Philippians 2:13). We have every reason to obey joyfully—and no true Christian will ever think of obedience as something optional.

We are not under law, but under grace. Far from being a manifesto for antinomianism or an authorization for licentious behavior, however, that important truth teaches us that both our justification and our obedience must properly be grounded in Christ and what He has done for us, rather than in ourselves and what we do for God.

The doctrine of justification by faith therefore provides the highest, purest incentive for

Christian obedience. As Paul wrote to the Romans, the mercies God displays in our justification provide all the reason we need to yield ourselves to Him as living sacrifices (Romans 12:1). Freed from the penalty of the law—loosed from the threat of condemnation for our disobedience—we are thus empowered by grace to surrender to God in a way we were powerless to do as unbelievers. And that is why the Christian life is continually portrayed in Scripture as a life of obedience.

No, obedience is not an issue of legalism, as many in our libertine age would have us believe; it is an issue of love—loving God as He commands us to do by doing what He commands—and we do so because we love Him so.

The Obedience of Faith

John Armstrong

The relationship between faith and obedience
has perennially prompted serious debate in the
Christian church. This was true, historically, in
the great sixteenth-century debate between the
Protestant Reformers and the Roman Catholic
theologians, who reacted to the Reformers' doctrine at the Council of Trent. This relationship
remains very much at the heart of modern
Christian teaching, be it evangelical or Catholic.
What is the biblical relationship of faith in the
promises of God to personal obedience to the
will of God as revealed in Scripture?

It seems that clear definitions of saving faith
are few and far between in the modern era. Even
fewer clear definitions are at hand regarding the
proper relationship of God-given faith to human obedience. On the one hand, modern evangelicals, in insisting properly that faith and
obedience are not the same, collapse faith and
works into one another, virtually making them
synonymous. In this approach no distinction of
any consequence is made between faith and
obedience. On the other hand, a large number

of modern teachers have argued, at least in principle, that faith and obedience have no *necessary* or intrinsic relationship; thus they are virtually exclusive of one another. In this pattern, which generally results in aberrant practice, people believe in Christ and His gospel, but for all practical purposes never really seem interested in the kind of evangelical obedience that *necessarily* follows true faith.

Texts which show the vital link between faith and evangelical obedience abound in the New Testament. For all practical purposes these texts are either ignored or misinterpreted by countless numbers of those who see no necessary relationship between saving faith and obedience. Paul, in a primary example of the type of text that I have in mind, writes: "But by the grace of God I am what I am, and His grace to me was not without effect. No, I worked harder than all of them—yet not I, but the grace of God that was with me" (1 Corinthians 15:10). No room here for a faith that does not obey!

Perhaps the most straightforward link between faith and obedience in Paul's writings can be seen in these familiar words:

> Therefore, my dear friends, as you have always obeyed—not only in my presence,

but now much more in my absence—
continue to work out your salvation with
fear and trembling, for it is God who
works in you to will and to act according
to his good purpose (Philippians 2:12–
13).

Surely, even the most cursory reading of
these verses should convince one not already
prejudiced otherwise that there is a faith, a vital
and living faith, and that this faith is intimately
and directly linked to obedience. As Luther, the
great champion of *sola fide,* often put it,
Christ's salvation comes to those who believe
the gospel on the basis of faith alone (cf.
Romans 4:5), but the faith which believes the
gospel is never *alone.* To believe is to be transformed by and through living faith. Indeed, the
central emphasis of the New Testament insists
upon this—living faith brings one into vital
union with Christ who is daily transforming
the one who believes.

Here I will focus upon this vital connection
between faith and obedience, which is grounded
in our union with Christ. I will direct your
thinking to perhaps the most seminal text regarding this relationship in the entire New Testament. What is particularly interesting about
this approach is that I take my argument

entirely from Paul's magnum opus regarding *sola gratia* and *sola fide*, i.e., the Epistle to the Romans. I plan to show that trust (faith) and obedience (works) are essentially and necessarily related in Paul's mind. Further, I will seek to show that this relationship actually forms the *essential core* of Pauline thought in terms of how he presents the gospel to a people he had never personally met.

It has been said many times that the grandest movements of reformation and heaven-sent revival have come when the great themes of Roman's have been preached with renewed clarity and power. If I am correct in understanding the matter before us in this present volume, then we desperately need to recover the correct relationship of faith to obedience. If we would see a new reformation those who preach desperately need this clarity.

The Function of the "Obedience of Faith"

In Paul's opening greetings to the Roman Christians, just after he identifies himself and his commission, he states his goal by writing: "Through Him and for His name's sake, we received grace and apostleship to call people from among all the Gentiles to the obedience that comes from faith" (Romans 1:5).

The phrase "the obedience that comes from faith," or, more simply, "the obedience of faith," is a unique Pauline construction, occurring only here, and later in the same epistle in a somewhat different form (cf. 16:25–26). What he has in mind, as we shall soon uncover, is what I will call "believing obedience," or "faith's obedience." His motive is said to be "for His (i.e., Christ's) name's sake." One may properly conclude that "the totality of Paul's missionary endeavors is epitomized by these words."[1] As has been noted, Paul's statement has to do with a comprehensive missionary vision which plainly corresponds to faith's obedience, or the kind of believing that always results, *necessarily*, in obedience.

We have noted that this same phrase occurs again at the end of this same letter:

> Now to Him who is able to establish you by my gospel and the proclamation of Jesus Christ, according to the revelation of the mystery hidden for long ages past, but now revealed and made known through the prophetic writings by the command of the eternal God, so that all nations might believe and obey him—to the only wise God be glory forever through Jesus Christ! Amen (Romans 16:25–27).

The phrase "believe and obey Him" is virtually the same phrase which occurs in Romans 1:5, and is, therefore, most likely a reference to the same "obedience of faith" as in 1:5. Therefore, the same phrase which guides Paul's intention in writing the introduction is central to the conclusion and doxology. I believe that within the use and meaning of this one little phrase, which I hope to demonstrate is intentionally ambiguous, lies a kind of grammatical and linguistic key to the thought of the entire epistle.

It has been properly noted that this phrase, in context, has an important eschatological significance as well.

> Analogous to 1:5, faith's obedience on the part of the Gentiles is the goal to which the revelation of the mystery looked. Consequently, faith and the obedience of faith assume a distinctively eschatological character. Seen in this light, "the obedience of faith" is to be regarded as a phrase of some significance for the understanding of Paul. It is, in other words, *his own articulation of the design and purpose of his missionary labors:* God is now bringing His purposes to pass in salvation history through Paul's gospel, i.e., the preaching of Jesus Christ (v. 25). Paul's commis-

sion, therefore, is to be viewed as nothing less than the eschatological actualization of the eternal plan to create faith's obedience among the nations.[2]

But what is the exact meaning and epistolary significance of "the obedience of faith" for the relationship of true faith to evangelical obedience? To this question we turn our attention.

The Relationship of Faith to Obedience

The precise question is: "What is the relationship between faith and obedience?" I am suggesting that this vital phrase, central to Paul's whole missionary endeavor and goal, is at the very heart of a correct answer to this question. Furthermore, I am submitting that here lies a key not always observed in the phrase "the obedience of faith."

Commentators have disagreed significantly regarding the exact range of meanings to be associated with the phrase "the obedience of [NIV: 'that comes from'] faith." There are two primary ways in which this phrase has been interpreted. Both make significant contributions to the proper exegesis of the verse, but neither do full justice to what I hope to show is a richer and more contextually accurate understanding of the phrase and its use.

1. The Obedience Which Comes from *Faith*

First, this phrase could be interpreted as referring to the obedience that faith produces, or in which faith results. The word "faith" here is a noun in the genitive case. This is the case of definition, source, or description. Greek grammarians agree that this generally makes a noun to function in some kind of adjectival manner. Here the commentators disagree as to whether or not the word "faith" (in the genitive case) functions in a subjective or objective manner.

Arguments for the objective genitive here are not as strong as those for the subjective. The subjective view reasons that what Paul has in mind is either "the obedience which faith works" or "the obedience which is required by faith." The real intention of both these options is that obedience finds its true fountainhead in faith. Though this is true, it does not encompass the full meaning of this phrase.

The simple truth of the exegetical issue at hand, as Douglas Moo has properly seen, is that "The genitive *pisteos* is hard to pin down."[3] If the faith in view here is *subjective,* then it could be translated as "the obedience which springs from faith." This view is held by a number of important commentators. William Hendriksen is illustrative of this position:

> The purpose for which Paul was appointed was to bring about obedience of faith. Such obedience is based on faith and springs from faith. In fact, so very closely are faith and obedience connected that they may be compared to inseparable identical twins. When you see one you see the other. A person cannot have genuine faith without having obedience, nor vice versa.[4]

F. F. Bruce, another exegete who holds the subjective genitive view, concludes that "the faith here is not the gospel, the body of doctrine presented for belief, but *the belief itself* (cf. Romans 15:18; 16:26)."[5]

Charles Hodge, nineteenth-century Princeton theologian, wrote:

> The subjective sense of *pistis* [faith] in the New Testament is so predominant that it is safest to retain it in this passage. The obedience of faith is that obedience which consists in faith, or of which faith is the controlling principle. The design of his apostleship was to bring all nations so to believe in Christ the Son of God that they should be entirely devoted to his service.

> The sense is the same if pistis [faith] be
> taken objectively, understood, however,
> not of the gospel, but of the inward
> principle of faith to which the nations
> were to be obedient.[6]

In this understanding of faith the emphasis
is clearly placed directly upon post-conversion
commitment, i.e., averring that the fruit which
properly *follows* saving faith will be evidenced
in obedience. This conclusion is surely accurate,
but I believe Paul is saying much more.

2. The Obedience Which Is Directed toward Faith

This view treats faith as a genitive of apposition. It is to be read as "the obedience directed
toward, or in [the] faith," in which case *pistis*
(faith) could refer to "a body of doctrine or to
the message of the gospel [itself]."[7] This would
translate the genitive as "the obedience which
consists in faith." Douglas Moo notes further
that a popular version of this idea, held by several important commentators as diverse as
Calvin, Nygren, and Cranfield, is the so-called
"epexegetical view" which translates the phrase
as "the obedience which *is* faith." C. E. B. Cranfield, who has done significant scholarly work
on Romans, writes:

> We take "of faith" to be what grammarians
> call a genitive of apposition. This seems
> more likely to be right than any of the
> other suggestions which have been made
> as, for example, that it means "required by
> faith" or that it is simply adjectival so
> equivalent to "believing."[8]

Support for this approach to the meaning of faith can be seen in the various texts where obedience and faith actually occur together in this epistle.

One important pair of passages that illustrates this point is Romans 1:8 and 16:19. In 1:8 Paul writes, "I thank my God through Jesus Christ for all of you, because your faith is being reported all over the world." In the parallel text of Romans 16:19, he says, "Everyone has heard about your obedience, so I am full of joy over you. . . ." Here the faith of the Roman believers, which is widely known, is equated with their obedience, which is equally known. Similar parallels can be demonstrated in Romans 10:16a and 10:16b, as well as in 11:23 with 11:30–31.

Furthermore, Paul plainly speaks of "obeying" the gospel. This is what prompts John Calvin to note correctly that "Faith is properly that by which we obey the Gospel."[9]

I add several other voices to build the case
for this understanding. D. Martyn Lloyd-Jones
wrote:

> The Apostle says . . . "the obedience of
> faith" in order to bring out this point—
> that he is talking about an obedience
> which consists in faith, or, if you like, an
> obedience of which faith is the central
> principle.[10]

The late professor John Murray noted:

> It is . . . intelligible and suitable to take
> "faith" as in apposition to "obedience" and
> understand it as the obedience which
> consists in faith. Faith is regarded as an
> act of obedience, or commitment to the
> gospel of Christ.[11]

To receive the gospel is to act in obedience to
the commandment of God who requires all to
repent and believe. The appositive view of Professor Murray acknowledges this well.

In a work from the last century, Robert
Haldane concluded:

> The gospel reforms those who believe it;
> but it would be presenting an imperfect
> view of the subject to say that it was

given to reform the world. It was given
that men might believe and be saved. The
obedience, then, here referred to, signifies
submission to the doctrine of the
gospel.[12]

All of this points out the tragedy of much
modern preaching. We often hear faith offered
to people as something that is (in our opinion)
good for them. It will bring happiness and
peace to their lives. We reason, therefore, that
we must encourage them to believe, even
though they have perfect freedom to say "No!"
We demonstrate this false idea when we make
silly statements such as "The Holy Spirit is a
gentleman and will not force you to believe the
gospel!" Or, "Christ knocks patiently at the
door of your heart, but will not come in unless
you open the door. He respects your choice too
much to do anything but knock, so you must
make the next move!" All of this prompts
James M. Boice to observe that with a framework like this one "sin becomes little more
than bad choices, and faith only means beginning to see the issues clearly."[13]

What is missing in most of these contemporary statements is the simple—but profoundly
important—truth that sin is primarily rebellion against God. It is, in one word, *disobedi-*

ence! Indeed, unbelief is itself massive disobedience, as the entire Gospel of John makes clear. We conclude, then, that the message of the gospel must be preached as a command, not merely as an offer. This idea seems clearly to be in Paul's mind when he puts the "obedience of faith" in the context of his own role as a faithful ambassador to the nations.[14]

The same idea is captured in Paul's sermon to the Athenians:

> In the past God overlooked such ignorance, but now He commands all people everywhere to repent. For He has set a day when He will judge the world with justice by the man He has appointed. He has given proof to all men by raising Him from the dead (Acts 17:30–31).

Massive evidence of weakness exists in the contemporary evangelical church because we do not present the gospel as a command from God. We trivialize the work of evangelism when we treat the gospel as a message that helps people "put their lives together," and leads them into an abundant life in which they can now "live happily ever after."

An Alternative Reading of Faith and Obedience

The subjective option, as noted above, tends to place too much emphasis on post-conversion obedience alone. The more objective option, as seen in its best expressions in what has been called the "epexegetical view," can too easily miss other important considerations that need to be more carefully noted. Douglas Moo helpfully summarizes my own sense of how these two views interact and why an alternative understanding is to be preferred. Moo observes:

> Paul's task was to call men and women to submission to the lordship of Christ (cf. 4b and 7b), a submission that began with conversion but which was to continue in a deepening, life-long commitment. This obedience to Christ as Lord is always closely related to faith, both as an initial, decisive step of faith and as a continuing "faith" relationship with Christ. In light of this, we understand the words *hypakoe* [obedience] and *pisteos* [faith] to be mutually interpreting: obedience always involves faith, and faith always involves obedience. They should not be equated, compartmentalized, or made into separate stages of Christian experience.[15]

Paul is *not* saying that faith plus "observing

(i.e., works of) the law" (cf. Galatians 2:16; 3:2, etc.) justifies the sinner before God. Neither the performance of ritual (ceremony), even ritual ordained by God (i.e. baptism and the Lord's Supper), nor the covenantal keeping of the law itself can *bring* one into relationship with God or *keep* one in relationship with God.

But Paul is not saying that one can believe without obedience, or that the necessity of faithfulness to the God of the covenant is somehow optional. Paul called men and women to a faith in Jesus Christ which was conceived of as *inseparably connected with* obedience to God and the covenant. The Savior to whom believing worshipers come is the Lord Jesus Christ. So-called "non-lordship" teachers are prone to suggest that we come to Jesus as God (i.e., deity) and that this has nothing to do with our submitting to Him as our Lord (in terms of resolve and commitment to follow). In reality, this explanation begs the question, for if you come to Jesus as God then you must truly respond to Jesus, in faith, as Jehovah God. To do this obviously implies that you submit.

We can only come to Christ in faith, not by "what our guilty hands have done." But the faith with which we come is clearly joined to an obedience that God grants to those who come believing. Further, we can only obey Jesus as Lord, day by day, when we continually give ourselves to him in faith. Adds Moo,

> Viewed in this light, the phrase ["the obedience of faith"] captures the full dimension of Paul's apostolic task, a task that was not confined to initial evangelization but that included also the building up and firm establishment of churches.[16]

The distinctions that Paul makes in his argument

> . . . are between the righteous and the wicked, believers and unbelievers, the obedient and the disobedient. These are the distinctions which constitute the contours of Paul's gospel, that gospel of God's righteousness with which he had been commissioned to bring about the obedience of faith for Christ's sake among the nations.[17]

It is interesting that Cranfield, a champion of the genitive of apposition which has been noted (i.e., "the obedience which consists in faith"), must also concede:

> It is also true to say that to make the decision of faith is an act of obedience toward

God and also that true faith by its very nature includes in itself the sincere desire
and will to obey God in all things.[18]

Professor John Murray concludes that the
implications are

. . . far-reaching. For the faith which the
apostleship was intended to promote was
not an evanescent act of emotion but the
commitment of whole-hearted devotion to
Christ and to the truth of His gospel. It is
to such faith that all nations are called.[19]

All this is a way of saying, in effect, that "the
obedience which consists in faith cannot be
abstracted from the obedience demanded by the
gospel."[20]

The phrase "the obedience of faith" appears,
after all, to be quite ambiguous. At the very
least it is not a simple phrase. This should
make the exegete cautious. It seems to me that
a case can be made for meaning *both* "the
obedience which *consists* in faith" and "the
obedience which is the *product* of faith."

What all of this ultimately means is that
most of the views generally taken of this text
are too restrictive. Consequently, a translation
like "faith's obedience" (or "believing obedi-

ence") seems better to preserve the studied ambiguity of Paul. This translation actually retains the ambiguity and honors the way in which Paul connects faith and obedience throughout the epistle.

What About Sola Fide?

Faith, throughout Paul's letter, begins as hearing the gospel and as trusting in the one promised to those who believe. But faith never ends there. Faith is dynamic and living. It always brings the believing one into living union with Christ Jesus who is Lord. "The word [faith] implies the submission of total personal response of the believer to the risen Lord." This "commitment factor" demonstrates that Paul's primary concern for the Roman believers was their perseverance in true faith.[21]

The discerning evangelical reader, who knows something of the history of the Protestant-Catholic debate regarding grace and faith, may object: "Doesn't this understanding of faith and obedience compromise the truth of *sola gratia* and *sola fide*?" I do not think so.

The late theologian G. C. Berkouwer, who observed that the phrase "the obedience of faith" actually gives us a hint of the nature of true faith, adds:

This obedience cannot be abstracted from
Him to whom the believer subjects himself. We cannot close our eyes to the element of obedience in faith, but if we see it
aright we shall realize that it serves to
show us how completely faith is directed
to its object.[22]

Don Garlington has wonderfully understood
the essence of this pregnant phrase for a fuller
New Testament theology:

. . . although the phrase "the obedience of
faith" occurs but twice (or once) in the
whole Pauline corpus, it comprises the
beginning, the middle, and the end of
Paul's preaching. As viewed within this
context of his missionary outreach, "the
obedience of faith" is a compendious way
of calling to mind the necessity of initial
faith, persevering faith, and the faith
which justifies in the last judgment. In
this light, ["the obedience of faith"] forms
the complement of "the righteousness of
God" as revealed ["from faith to faith"]
(Rom. 1:17). In short, "the obedience of
faith" concentrates into one short sequence of words the essence of Paul's
gospel of salvation for the world.[23]

Paul is demonstrating in Roman's how the
Gentiles, who do not have the law and the

covenants, have actually come into covenantal relationship with the God of Israel through believing the gospel, and thus have entered into the obedience of the one new Man (cf. Romans 5:12–21). Through union with this Man, those who believe have also come into vital relationship with God Himself. This union results in faithfulness to God through the new covenant. And this faithfulness is "obedience," or, as I am calling it for the sake of clarification, "evangelical obedience."

By the use of the word "evangelical" I mean to underscore that this "obedience" is not the obedience of the flesh, or the "obedience" of our efforts to keep the demands of the law as the grounds of our acceptance with God. But "is our future and final justification before God on the last day based in any way upon our law-keeping?" This is, as I understand it, the central question of the Reformation, though Luther did not always state it in exactly this way. He was concerned to know if a believer can know assurance of *final* pardon. Can I know that I have the "righteousness of God," so that I might stand absolved of all my sins, clothed in the perfect righteousness which God will accept on the last day?

To speak of obedience as *necessary* and as

vitally connected to faith makes it sound, to some, as if obedience actually *adds* something to the justification of God. I answer: obedience is itself the product of faith, when it is based upon the gospel, and where true faith exists there will be—indeed, there *must* be—both present and final justification by God. I believe that Don Garlington gives us the proper caution when he concludes, "When cause and effect are thus kept in proper sequence, any initial anxiety at the notion of justification by 'doing' should be ameliorated, if not quelled altogether."[24]

God will not, at the end of the age, judge the believer on the basis of how many good works he has done, but upon whether or not he was actually clinging to Christ alone for the righteousness of God. But still, you may object, "How can I know that I am clinging to Christ? What if my faith is not the faith of obedience?" Doesn't the idea of obedience and perseverance being vitally linked with faith actually destroy assurance and Christian security?

Assurance?
It must first be seen that real warnings are given to all believers in the New Testament. These warnings are addressed to those who give

all outward appearance of being united to
Christ. These warnings must be taken seriously. Indeed, in the New Testament, taking
these seriously leads to a great end—namely,
standing in faith. Many modern notions of
eternal security clearly fail to take these warnings seriously. Simply put, not all who profess
to have faith in Christ have "the obedience of
faith." There is a faith, mentioned quite often in
the New Testament, that falls short of saving
faith. Judas had such faith. Others who possessed this type of faith are frequently named
in Paul's own letters. Paul's warnings, contained
in a phrase like "the obedience of faith," are actually "directed not at those who, out of weakness and vulnerability, commit sins, but [rather
they are aimed at those who] are puffed up,
guilty of presumption, and living in a state of
illusion."[25] Believers sin and believers fail, often
out of profound human weakness. But believers
keep on believing and thereby cling to Christ in
His covenant. They live as those who are
faithful to the God who has shown them grace
and mercy. They experience the work of the
Spirit actually producing in them the kind of
faith in view here in Romans 1.

What then do these warnings actually mean
for the assurance of faith? I believe Paul appro-

priately answers this question when he writes: "But the gift is not like the trespass. For if the many died by the trespass of the one man, how much more did God's grace and the gift that came by the grace of the one man, Jesus Christ, overflow to the many" (Romans 5:15). "The gift of God is eternal life in Christ Jesus our Lord" (Romans 6:23). G. C. Berkouwer, in his classic work on perseverance (which personally sustained my own soul during the days which surrounded the death of my own father), puts this relationship well when he says, "Faith knows the prevenience of God's grace and the gift of perseverance, which is identical with the act of God's preservation, because through grace the transition from death unto life is irreversible."[26] This is, after all, the correct approach to a settled assurance.

Even when the Apostle exhorts believers to examine their faith, which he plainly does (cf. 2 Corinthians 13:5), it should be noted that he urges them to see if they are holding to faith, *not* to works. This appeal demonstrates that we do not primarily gain assurance by looking at our works. We gain and keep a strong assurance by looking at Christ with the faith that vitally gazes at His glory and completed work. We remember that He is even now interceding for us, and bearing in His own body the marks of our redemption.

Further, the pastoral method utilized by Paul in this regard is worthy of careful note. Paul writes: "Not that we lord it over your faith, but we work with you for your joy, because it is *by faith that you stand firm* (2 Corinthians 1:24). Many modern pastors, in coming to understand warning passages, and the relationship between faith and obedience as outlined above, cease to labor for the joy of their hearers and actually cause men and women to stand on the basis of something other than *faith*.

Enter Exhibit A: Martin Luther

But what about *sola fide*? Should we still speak of a salvation that is *all* of grace and appropriated by faith *alone*? Throughout this chapter we have seen a definitive relationship between what we properly call justification and sanctification. The initiative in salvation is God's, yet *response* to this initiative in grace is also part of the saving work of Christ. This is what God does in giving His Spirit to those whom He graciously chooses to redeem. It is the Spirit of life who empowers and enables the believing one both to come in faith and remain in faith. A more Trinitarian conception of salvation would secure our thought against a number of false ideas.

Luther and other Reformers were responding to the introduction of the concept of personal merit into justification. In the Middle Ages the focus of much scholastic theology had been placed upon how the individual could appropriate the grace of God. What developed over several centuries was a concept that if you did the best that you could to come to God your effort would be *rewarded* with enough grace to help you take the further steps that would eventually bring you home to the Father. (Historical theologians speak of this view, properly, as a confusion of justification as a finished legal act, and sanctification as a process of growth and obedience. Rome retains this same confusion right down to the present time, as can be seen in the modern *Catechism of the Catholic Church*.)

For several centuries leading up to Luther's time, Mass and penance were the answers the church gave to the question of "How can I really come home to God?" What Luther discovered was that the righteousness of God, which man must have if he would be forgiven and accepted, comes *not* by human efforts, but "by faith from first to last" (cf. Romans 1:17).

Luther's salvation and ultimate freedom came from understanding that grace came not to human effort and striving—albeit through sacraments and the life of the church—but to faith alone. He understood receiving grace as truly believing the promises held out to sinners in the gospel.[27]

As long as *sola fide* is understood in this context, which has not always been the case even on the Protestant side of this debate, it is a proper and sound affirmation.[28] However, when justification is not considered in its larger New Testament context, problems inevitably arise because we do not give proper attention to the teaching of the Bible itself. Let me explain.

"The Righteousness of God" Alone

The New Testament does not contain, as such, a doctrine of justification by faith alone. What we actually have is a doctrine of the righteousness of God alone, under which the historically debated doctrine of justification by faith alone should be subsumed. This is why we should stress that "we [should] press on to speak more particularly of the relation of righteousness to the last judgment."[29] Because God's righteousness is the sole need of sinners, the issue in the New Testament is really

"Where do we get this required righteousness?" The answer, both in the Reformers and
in the Bible, is that we get this righteousness in
Christ alone. Even historically, I would argue,
solus Christus was a vital issue. *Sola gratia* and
sola fide were understood, in essence, to
protect this central truth—that salvation is
found in "no other name under heaven." You
must be saved by Christ alone (i.e., directly),
not by or through the church, its sacraments,
or anything you bring to the work of grace.

Much of the problem in this debate is that
we get locked into historical categories. These
need to be considered as part of God's providence and care for the truth, but at the same
time we miss some of the significant exegetical
categories that are revealed in the New Testament itself.

The historic and current dichotomy between
faith and works, both in the popular arena and
in the field of Pauline scholarship, has often
been badly stated precisely because too sharp a
contrast has been made to exist

> . . . between the grace of God on the one
> hand, and human achievement as the
> ground or instrument of justification on
> the other. *Faith* and *works* are in this
> sense mutually exclusive. But the apostle

expects that faith will work through love (Gal. 5:6), while he conjoins "faith" and "work" in one of his first references to 'faith' (*pistis*), viz. 1 Thess. 1:3 (in fact the very first instance if 1 Thessalonians is Paul's first letter).[30]

It is genuinely difficult, as the above statement suggests, to understand how and why Paul could put "works" and "faith" together, as he does in the aforementioned Thessalonian passage, if these ideas are as dichotomous as many propose. They are clearly placed together in the very same phrase because they are, as I have argued, *indispensably* and *intimately* connected. To use an apt phrase from a different context: "What God has joined together, let no one put asunder."

Our True Basis of Standing Before God

In the more traditional understanding of *sola fide* it is often said that Christians appropriate to themselves the righteousness of God on the basis of faith. The more Pauline way of understanding this should add that *in Christ* we are brought into a vital union wherein we share in His covenantal loyalty, which was previously God's alone. In this covenantal relationship, based solely on union with Christ, the righteousness of God "communicated to Christians is nothing more or less than the ongoing righteousness of Christ, the continuing obedience of the one just man, lived out now in Christians and forming the basis of their destiny to eternal life."[31]

Steve Motyer has stated well this decidedly more Christocentric understanding of the righteousness of God and its relationship to our justification and salvation. He writes:

> The basis of the whole life of the people of God is His righteousness—His outreaching, saving mercy which rescues His creation for Himself. This righteousness has now been supremely expressed in Christ. But as men are grasped by it, "justified" and made acceptable to God, so they are stamped with the image of their righteous Savior, and summoned to live in imitation of Him as His people.[32]

In all of this I must plead for a balanced application of the conclusions made in this chapter. It must be stated and restated, because of our propensity to confusion in this, that there is absolutely *no* possibility of a "righteousness by works" (cf. Romans 5:15–17; 6:23). In this sense, *sola fide* is properly defended, and stands to this day, as the "rising or falling of the true church" (Luther). The gift-character of God's righteousness in Christ alone excludes *any* moral achievement or human boasting. There is nothing that we bring to God's reconciling, saving work in Christ except our sinful lives. For this reason the common justification/sanctification model is still useful with its stress upon the fact that salvation is all of God.

At the same time we need to consider with John Murray's insights that, since the New Testament usage of sanctification normally speaks not so much of a process as of a once-for-all act, we must conclude (as Garlington puts it) that, "In this light, it is difficult to think that 'justification' and 'sanctification' are radically distinct, inasmuch as both, in their dominant New Testament employment, have reference to the same event." By this I mean that both of these doctrines have reference to the "outworking of 'the righteousness of God,' commencing with the vindication/rightwising of the believer in Christ and eventuating in eternal life."[33]

Ordo Salutis?
Protestant Reformed thinking has tended to speak of an *ordo salutis,* or "an order of salvation." This conception has had its own useful-

ness in terms of protecting the *sola gratia* nature of salvation in the sovereignty of God. At the same time, several modern Reformed theologians have properly criticized several aspects of this traditional framework on more exegetical grounds.

Richard B. Gaffin has suggested that the *ordo salutis* is devoid of the eschatological context of Paul's thought. Gaffin wishes to stress that in Paul soteriology *is* eschatology in a very real way. All salvation experience, in Gaffin's understanding, is rooted in solidarity with Christ's resurrection and the coming new creation inaugurated by that resurrection. Garlington adequately reflects Gaffin's concern when he concludes:

> Thus, this understanding of present Christian experience as an eschatological tension between resurrection realized and resurrection yet to be is totally foreign to the *ordo salutis*, for which the categories of justification, adoption, sanctification, and regeneration are *deprived of any eschatological significance and any really integral connection with the future.*[34]

Gaffin suggests, second, that the *ordo salutis* concept generally treats justification, adoption, and sanctification as separate acts. Yet, Gaffin properly observes, Paul treats these not so much as distinctive acts, but as *distinct aspects* of a *single saving act*. The most problematic part of all in the *ordo salutis* concept is the way in which the problem of faith and obedience is related to the larger whole of our actual union with Christ. Garlington is right when he concludes that "if these other acts are in some sense prior to union with Christ, then that union is improperly subordinated to them and its *biblical* significance severely attentuated."[35]

The late Reformed theologian Anthony A. Hoekema was another who called into question the *ordo salutis* idea by suggesting that further thought and work were needed in light of biblical concerns regarding God's work of saving sinners. He noted the following important concerns that have profoundly shaped my own thought in regard to this matter:

> 1. The terms used in the *ordo salutis* conception (regeneration, conversion, renewal, etc.) are not used in the Bible in the *same way* as theologians have often used them;
> 2. The order often given for these doctrines in God's salvation is not the order cited by the scripture at several points (e.g., 1 Cor. 6:11);
> 3. The primary text often cited for an

ordo salutis conception is Romans 8:30, which simply does not have as its primary purpose steps in the order of salvation as normally presented by systematic theologians;

4. Faith must never be understood as *one* stage in the order of salvation, since faith must be exercised throughout the whole of the Christian's life;

5. Justification and sanctification are not successive stages in the Christian life, but are simultaneous [both numbers 4 and 5 are crucial insights which reflect much of the view taken by me in this chapter]; and,

6. Finally, the order suggested by various theologians leaves out several parts of the Biblical doctrine of salvation that are vital, e.g., love and hope.[36]

Categories such as regeneration, justification, and sanctification are distinct and useful for careful thought, but we must keep in mind that these distinct entities can never be separated. We do much better to think of salvation not so much in terms of order (since even here we are not exactly sure of God's mind or timing), but rather in terms of a pathway—a pathway in which there are various distinguishable aspects. Anthony Hoekema helps us think more biblically by suggesting that salvation is better conceived of not so much as a line with successive steps or stages (i.e., regeneration, conversion, justification, sanctification, perseverance,), but rather as a pentagonal building whose five walls are constructed of experiences which begin and continue *simultaneously*.

Conclusion

Hoekema draws out the implications of this way of thinking about salvation. Regeneration must occur, for example, at the beginning of our relationship with Christ. But it does not end there. Its effects continue in that the person who is regenerate lives a regenerate lifestyle. Although faith and repentance are at the beginning of the Christian's journey, both must continue throughout the whole. Martin Luther understood this matter of repentance being lifelong when in the first of his famous *Ninety-Five Theses* he wrote: "When our Lord and Master Jesus Christ said 'repent,' He meant that the entire life of believers should be one of repentance." What this means is that repentance "can never be reduced to a single act that stands alone at the beginning of the Christian life, nor can it be understood superficially and one-dimensionally."[37] Calvin speaks in this way as well, and refers to the fact that our union with Christ must result in what he calls "mortification and vivification." Justification does occur when one accepts Christ by faith, but this is followed by a lifelong appropriation of its gracious benefits. Sanctification occurs over the course of an entire lifetime, and is completed only after death; therefore perseverance in faith and repentance (expressed in evangelical obedience) is necessary for the whole of one's Christian life.

Another way of saying all of this is to understand that these various aspects of God's salvation by grace are interactive. Faith is not a one-time means of receiving justification, as is sometimes understood in the immeasurable practical errors that abound in our day. Faith is, rather, a necessity throughout the person's whole life. It is, as the Reformed tradition has always insisted, *impossible* to be justified without also being sanctified. Another way of saying this is to insist that if you are regenerated you will also persevere in the very faith given to you by the active working of the Spirit.

Finally, as believers we must recognize that we remain in the already/not yet tension between this age and one to come. This is the eschatological dimension of "the obedience of

faith" that I have sought to emphasize throughout. Those who believe are already in Christ, as
righteous in a certain sense as they ever will be.
At the same time these same "righteous" believers are not yet perfect. Believers are on the road
that leads to the glory to come, but they have
not reached that glory. Therefore, Hoekema is
surely correct when he concludes that believers
are "*genuinely* new persons but not yet *totally
new*" (italics in original).[38]

The person who has faith in Christ will experience persistent conflict throughout the en-
tirety of this life. He will also, according to the
realism of Paul's epistle to the Romans (cf.
Romans 7) know periodic defeat. Perfection, as
well as any conception of salvation that can be
grounded in human merit, is ruled out completely. Finally, by the grace of God alone, by
(through) believing obedience (or faith's obedience), those who entrust themselves to Christ
alone will be "more than conquerors through
Him who loved us" (Romans 8:37).

---

[1] Don B. Garlington, *Faith, Obedience and Perseverance.* Paul
Siebeck (Tubingen, Germany: J. C. B Mohr, 1994), 11.
[2] Garlington, *Faith,* p. 13 (emphasis in the original).
[3] Douglas Moo, *Romans 1–8: The Wycliffe Exegetical Commentary,*
(Chicago: Moody Press, 1991), p. 44.
[4] William Hendriksen, *Romans 1–8: The New Testament
Commentary* (Grand Rapids, Mich.: Eerdmans, 1980), p. 45.

[5] F. F. Bruce, *The Epistle of Paul to the Romans:* (Grand Rapids: Mich.: Eerdmans, 1963), p. 74.

[6] Charles Hodge, *Commentary on Romans* (Edinburgh: Banner of Truth, 1972 reprint edition), pp. 21-22.

[7] Moo, *Romans,* p. 44.

[8] Cranfield, *Romans: A Shorter Commentary* (Grand Rapids:, Mich.: Eerdmans, 1985), p. 8.

[9] John Calvin, *Commentary on Romans,* Beveridge Edition, Vol 19, Grand Rapids, Mich.: Baker, 1979 reprint, p. 18.

[10] D. Martyn Lloyd-Jones, *Romans: An Exposition of Chapter 1, The Gospel of God* (Grand Rapids, Mich.: Zondervan, 1985), pp. 137–38.

[11] John Murray, *The Epistle to the Romans* (Grand Rapids, Mich.: Eerdmans, 1968), p. 13.

[12] Robert Haldane, *An Exposition to the Romans* (MacDill AFB, Fla.: MacDonald, n.d.) pp. 30–31.

[13] James M. Boice, *Romans 1–4: An Expositional Commentary.* (Grand Rapids, Mich.: Baker, 1991), p. 55.

[14] Boice, *Romans 1–4,* p. 56.

[15] Moo, *Romans 1–8,* p. 44-45.

[16] Moo, *Romans 1–8,* p. 45.

[17] Glenn N. Davies, *Faith and Obedience in Romans: A Study in Romans 1-4* (Sheffield: Sheffield Academic Press, 1990), p. 19.

[18] C. E. B. Cranfield, *A Critical and Exegetical Commentary on the Epistle to the Romans* 2 vols. (Edinburgh: T. & T. Clark, 1979), 1:66–67.

[19] Murray, *Epistle to the Romans,* p. 14.

[20] Garlington, *Faith,* p. 17.

[21] Garlington, *Faith,* p. 31.

[22] G. C. Berkouwer, *Faith and Justification* (Grand Rapids, Mich.: Eerdmans, 1954), p. 195.

[23] Garlington, *Faith,* p. 145.

[24] Ibid., *Faith,* p. 147.

[25] Ibid., *Faith,* p. 147.

[26] Berkouwer, *Faith and Perseverance* (Grand Rapids, Mich.: Eerdmans, 1958), pp. 237-38.

[27] See John H. Armstrong, ed. *Roman Catholicism: Evangelical Protestants Analyze What Divides and Unites Us*; 1994. In chapter 2, D. Clair Davis, "How Did the Church in Rome Become Roman Catholicism?" demonstrates very clearly how this whole matter evolved. In chapter 3, Robert D. Godfrey, "What Caused the Great Divide?" shows how Luther came to believe and find peace.

[28] See Don Kistler, ed., *Justification By Faith ALONE!* (Morgan, Pa.: Soli Deo Gloria, 1994).

[29] Garlington, *Faith*, p. 153.

[30] D. A. Carson, ed., *Right With God* (Grand Rapids, Mich.: Baker, 1992), cf. P. T. O'Brien's chapter, "Some Crucial Issues of the Last Two Decades," 94.

[31] Garlington, *Faith*, p. 154.

[32] Steve Motyer, "Righteousness By Faith in the New Testament," in *Here We Stand: Justification By Faith Today* (London: Hodder & Stoughton, 1986), pp. 53–54.

[33] Garlington, *Faith*, p. 157.

[34] Garlington., *Faith*, p. 158 (italics in original).

[35] Garlington, *Faith*, p. 158 (italics in original).

[36] Anthony A. Hoekema, *Saved By Grace* (Grand Rapids, MIch.: Eerdmans, 1989), pp. 11–17. This is an excellent book that I have used profitably time and again as a text in teaching soteriology. I depend heavily upon it in the last paragraphs of this chapter. It properly considers the important Reformed and systematic categories of thought, as well as the historical debates and issues. At the same time it roots the doctrine of salvation profoundly in the exegesis of the text of Scripture.

[37] Sinclair B. Ferguson, "Recovery and Confession," in James M. Boice, ed. *Here I Stand: A Call from Confessing Evangelicals* (Grand Rapids, Mich.: Baker, 1996), in chapter six, "Recovery and Confession" by Sinclair B. Ferguson, p. 135.

[38] Hoekema, *Saved by Grace*, pp. 11–17.

Legalism and Antinomianism: Two Deadly Paths off the Narrow Road

Jonathan Gerstner

The final moment of history has occurred. The Lord has returned! The multitudes quake with fear, begging the mountains to fall upon them so that they may not face the impending wrath of the Lamb. Many, however, throng to see Christ, greeting Him not as a great teacher, but as who He truly is—the Lord. They have lived in joyful anticipation of this day, performing remarkable works of ministry in Christ's name. The Lord Jesus turns to this multitude of confessors with words which resound throughout the heavens and the earth: "Depart from Me, I never knew you."

This picture of the end times remains one of the most important lessons which the Lord taught His disciples. It appropriately comes at the end of the Sermon on the Mount, given in a special way to those who had endured His prior hard sayings and still were considering following Him. In addition to the many who will be lost and know it, when Christ returns there will be many lost who confidently rush to meet the One they consider their Lord.

The reality of this startling truth of Scripture has led some to conjecture that people can lose their salvation. Yet the truth is much more frightening than that theory. This very warning of Christ is not of apostasy. He will not say, "I knew you, but you drifted away." Rather will He say, "I *never* knew you. In all your life on this earth, in all your ministry in My name, I *never* knew you." Christ does not warn those He knows of the danger of departing. He warns His disciples to see if they are truly His disciples. One can do remarkable, even miraculous deeds in Christ's name, have a complete confidence that one is in a state of saving grace, be bold enough to greet Christ on Judgment Day, and never have a living relationship with Him.

This essay aims to address the theological foundations behind this sobering truth. There are two twin errors which open the door to this false assurance of the lost. Legalism involves the many ways in which individuals believe that their own moral actions are at least part of the ground for their right standing before God.

Legalism is a probable error of many in the group mentioned in the Sermon on the Mount, for they quickly remind Christ of the many actions they did in Christ's name. This implies a trust in these deeds as they stand in the presence of the Lord.

The opposite error is called antinomianism. This is the ideology that says a person may be right with God through a faith which does not transform one's life and produce good works. These condemned individuals were "workers of iniquity," those who lived in unrepentant sin.

Some defended the legitimacy of living in sin by twisting the doctrine of grace. They are antinomians. Others were legalists who believed their pious acts were part of their right standing with God and covered the remaining unrepented iniquity in their life. Legalists and antinomians met together to embrace Christ, only to be identified together as "workers of iniquity" and cast into outer darkness.

Throughout history these twin dangers have needed to be carefully examined and exposed. Precisely because these counterfeits live in the bosom of the church, they must be clearly demonstrated. However, today there is an unprecedented explosion of these errors among professing evangelicals. Pointing out the prevalent nature of these errors is a painful duty. We will examine abuses of the terms to clear those innocently accused. Yet men and women who have cast out demons and done many wonderful works in Christ's name will be found to defend a counterfeit gospel. I personally have been blessed by the writings and lectures of those who today defend another gospel, as I am sure believers in Paul's day had bittersweet memories of the early ministry of Demas. My deepest hope is that God will be glorified and in His mercy use this chapter to convict and convert famous and unknown persons alike that we may together rejoice on that day.

The Scandal of the Narrow Road

"Broad is the road that leads to destruction. Narrow is the road that leads to life and few they are that find it" (Matthew 7:13–14). Our Lord has a remarkable gift of "hard sayings." Few have been as devastating and hard to accept as this one about how unique the road to life truly is.

Obviously the doctrine of a narrow road does not appeal to those currently on the broad road. The gospel appears foolish to those who appreciate their multilane highway with room for all spiritual opinions.

Sadly this hard saying also has a tendency to trip those who consider themselves to be on the narrow way. There is an unyielding pressure in fallen man to desire to be in the majority. If any possible contortion can be made to squeeze more lanes onto the narrow way, it will be done.

Yet a narrow way it is, and so it will stay. God is holy; humans are sinners. There is no reason why God should provide any way to salvation. But in His infinite mercy, He provides one.

Jesus Christ alone is the Savior. But how does Christ save? If Christ were merely a good teacher, then many lanes could be found in the way of life. Fragments of His divine teaching remain in other religions and philosophies. However, the narrow way proclaims that Christ was the unique God-Man, fully God and fully man. He came to die, to be a sacrifice to turn God's wrath away from certain sinners.

How is the sacrifice applied to humans? If arbitrarily by God, apart from any secondary means, there would be no sense in our Lord's discussion of the two ways. God would direct the redemption apart from any human role at all, with no gate to enter nor need for pilgrims to walk on their journey.

But Scripture makes it very clear that the redemption purchased by Christ must be applied by His Spirit in life, in space and time, on this earth. The application of the redemption purchased by Christ is best summarized in the formula which my father, Dr. John H. Gerstner, so succinctly produced and which is recorded in his *Primer on Justification* (now joined with all his other primers in a work he called *Primitive Theology*, published by Soli Deo Gloria):

Faith → Justification + Works

A sinful person is made right in God's eyes only though faith. Passively he receives redemption by trusting that Christ has purchased this redemption for him. But that trust itself is born only by the Spirit of God opening the heart to believe, and that new heart given by the Spirit leads us instantaneously onward to seek to do works of gratitude in order to bring glory to the Lord who redeemed us.

There are two steep cliffs on either edge of the narrow way that leads to life. Both lead the follower crashing down in a fall that inexorably leads to destruction. Even those who do not follow that path themselves are in great danger of affirming the validity of the roads off the edge as in fact a part of the narrow way.

Legalism: The Ugly Bribe to the Holy Judge

The first lane of the broad path which pretends to be a part of the narrow way is legalism. Legalism must be very carefully defined. Legalism teaches that a person's right standing before God, and his receiving eternal life, are purchased fully or in part by the person's observance of the law. Man earns all or part of his redemption through his own good efforts.

Classic unadulterated legalism can best be represented by the formula:

Works → Justification - Faith

In other words, it doesn't matter what one believes; one will go to heaven if one does good works.

Liberal Christianity, that is, the ideology which claims to embrace Christianity while denying the miraculous events behind it, has championed this view. Good works, usually in the manner of striving after social justice, are the key to making an individual right with God.

Liberation theology has a much more serious emphasis on the role of Scripture than classic liberalism; nevertheless in practice it makes siding with the oppressed the key criterion for being right with God. My sojourn with the South African church in the twilight years of white rule uncovered frightening similarities in the two largest opposing camps then fighting for the soul of Christianity. On one side, many of the defenders of apartheid acted as if all persons defending this understanding of cultures were right with God, be they professing evangelicals or agnostics. On the other side, many viewed all who were opposed to the system as right in God's eyes, be they professing evangelical Christians or Muslims.

Serious emphasis on social and political issues in the church, without theological discernment, runs the risk of allowing the church's primary role as proclaimer of the gospel to be exchanged for the false gospel of legalism. The justifying good work becomes the issue of the day. As strongly as we must speak out against the societal evil of abortion, we would be naive to ignore that the contemporary prolife movement is certainly running that danger. Indeed, recent documents claiming spiritual unity between orthodox Roman Catholics and evangelicals would be inconceivable apart from the prolife movement and other efforts to promote moral values in society.

However, if one keeps the pure gospel foremost, one realizes that "whatever is not of faith is sin" (Romans 14:23). In other words, without

being right with God, all external morality is
not truly good. So one can legitimately work
with others of any faith to promote external or
civic righteousness, while being aware that no
degree of civic righteousness attainable by fallen
man makes a person right with God. Using
good works to justify oneself is as objectionable
to the Lord of heaven as a bribe is to an honest
judge. To add stupidity to malice, the legalist
tries to bribe the holy Judge with deeds that are
despicable to the Judge rather than alluring. All
his righteousness is as filthy rags (Isaiah 64:6).

One cannot help noting the unity between
other world religions and false or liberal
Christianity in their basic legalism. Although
none of these religions' followers will run to
embrace Christ as Lord on that final day, many
still anxiously await the redemption they are
purchasing by their actions. Muslims teach that
one is right with Allah through submission to
his will. Buddhism and Hinduism speak of
achieving liberation from this world of illusion
through living a selfless life. To the extent that
non-Christian religions speak of faith or right
doctrines, these carry value only as a type of
works. One brings his right understanding of
spiritual realities to the bar of redemption as
part of his generic morality. This road off the

edge has captured most of the world.

However, the more one encounters the typical unchurched person of the West, one finds that unadulterated legalism is alive and well among the irreligious as well. The Evangelism Explosion method has asked countless people the now-famous question, "If you were to die tonight and God were to ask you, 'Why should I let you into My heaven?' what would you say?" The overwhelming majority of those who have no relationship to any religion give some sort of a legalist answer. "I am a good person." "I try to live a moral life." "I have never hurt anyone." Deep in the fallen man's condition is the desire to earn his own redemption.

Part of this universal desire to redeem oneself by actions is an embedded nostalgia for the original relationship between God and humans. God created humanity in relationship with Him. Living a life of complete holiness, being human reflections of God's nature, would provide continuity of eternal life. This relationship, often called the "covenant of works," did link eternal life in God's presence with faithfulness to God's command and with reflecting His nature. In a central sense this covenant was never abrogated, for God's nature never changes. Christ can still tell the expert in the law, who foolishly thought he kept the commandments perfectly, "Do these things and you shall live" (Luke 10:28). The problem is not the God-given instinct that good deeds are a path to life; it is the horrendous failure to understand that in this fallen world "no one is good but God alone" (Matthew 19:17). "All have sinned and fall short of the glory of God" (Romans 3:23). In other words, any action short of perfect reflection of God's goodness is not truly good. Legalism is, at its root, failure to acknowledge one's own moral state.

Baptized Legalism: The Galatian Heresy

However, within the professing Christian community there is another invasion of legalism, more subtle than unadulterated legalism. This form of legalism still speaks of the essential character of faith in Christ, and can confuse many within the visible church. Its denial of the gospel comes from combining works with faith as the source of an individual's right standing with God:

Faith + Works ➜ Justification

This ancient error is the first recorded heresy of the New Testament, the Galatian heresy. The initial manifestation hinged on the role of the observance of the ceremonial law for a believer. The Galatian legalists were saying that one could not be right with God unless he was circumcised. Those, including some of their own number, who had thought they were right with God when they believed the gospel were sadly mistaken. Circumcision was a prerequisite to being right with God.

It is important to distinguish between the Galatian heresy and honest differences of opinion concerning the role of the ceremonial law for the believer. Paul himself circumcised Timothy at least partially so that he would not offend those believers who thought that circumcision was an important part of the life of gratitude of the believer. Paul was convinced rightly that circumcision had been fulfilled in baptism, which was the circumcision of Christ, and that baptized people did not need to be circumcised. But that internal Christian debate was of little importance to Paul, and he willingly had Timothy circumcised. However, when the legalists of Galatia claimed that circumcision is a prerequisite of one's right standing with God, Paul uncompromisingly declared the anathema upon them as lost deniers of the gospel. If any professing believer of the gospel agrees to circumcision in light of the teaching of these heretics, he has denied the gospel and is lost! Justification by faith is not the gospel. Justification by faith *alone* is the only gospel! The entire book of Galatians proves that the Bible teaches that faith alone is the only path of justification.

This heresy again raised its ugly head in the medieval church. Faith was still seen as essential; no one would be justified without faith. Faith and works cooperated in one's right standing. The beautiful passage on "faith working through love" (Galatians 5:6) was twisted to defend this heresy. This text from the heart of Paul's assault on the Galatian heresy clearly teaches orthodoxy: that the only faith that justifies is true faith, evidenced by its fruit of loving actions. However, those who twisted Paul, like the other Scriptures, to their own destruction claimed that faith and its loving actions together were the elements that purchased redemption.

This heresy began to gain an ever deeper hold on the medieval church. The invention of purgatory, a place where believers could complete the attainment of merit in God's eyes and be admitted to heaven, added more structure to the error. Similarly, penance, as behavior prescribed to gain God's approval, became a false sacrament of the false gospel. Penance historically had its root in the perceived need for external evidence of the sincerity of the person claiming repentance and faith. But, as with all extra-biblical church innovations, it quickly was used by the rising heresy.

The medieval heresy was a denial of the gospel in the heart of the church itself. Scripture condemned it as another gospel. It was also rejected by the early church fathers. When Luther and Zwingli, with the assistance of Augustine's writings, rediscovered the gospel, and started clearly to proclaim it and attack the externals which were inconsistent with the gospel, the nascent heresy became official. The Council of Trent affirmed once and for all that those who taught the gospel of justification by faith alone were damned, and the Roman Catholic Church formally affirmed that faith and works together are the ground of one's right standing with God. This heresy became "orthodoxy" for the largest part of professing Christians.

Contemporary Twists of Legalism

Contemporary professing evangelicals have seen some unique twists in legalism. The most pervasive and seductive ones are the often unconscious attempts to turn faith itself into a work. In a sense, all Arminian theories teaching that faith is a product of the human will, if consistently applied, would lead to the legalistic heresy. By a gracious act of God, it seems that many Arminians fail to work their doctrine of faith through to its consistent conclusion, and are saved as if by fire. However, some of the lost will be clinging to their own man-made faith on that last day when they rush to meet the Lord who never knew them.

A growing number of professing evangelicals are adopting a view of faith which is indisputably legalistic. Faith is, for them, clearly a matter of human effort, thus becoming itself a work, leading to the formula: works → justification. Extreme faith healers have described faith as something that a person must produce in order to be healed. If the individual allows himself to doubt that he is healed, he will lose his healing. Similarly, justifying faith must rest upon the efforts of the believer.

Most subtle of all is the trend among professing evangelicals to affirm that the heretical Galatian view of justification adopted by the Roman Catholic church is an acceptable Christian option. As long as faith is essential to justification, they argue, it need not be by faith alone.

The shocking document of 1994, *Evangelicals and Catholics Together* (ECT), made the claim that evangelicals and Roman Catholics are brothers in Christ. It states that both groups believe in justification by faith, and the key Tridentine citation of "faith working in love" is cited. The document is not speaking about the growing number of evangelicals who have confusedly stayed in the Roman Catholic church; the document unambiguously states that orthodox Roman Catholics and evangelicals are one in Christ. By God's grace, some of the professing evangelicals who signed the document have since repudiated their error; however, the majority have shamelessly continued to persevere and defend ECT in writing.

A significant subgroup of professing evangelicals among the ECT signers later wrote a clarifying document that affirmed their personal belief in justification by faith alone. This statement completely dodged the central concern. The question is not whether some of the signers themselves believed in justification by faith alone. The question is whether they continue to affirm with ECT that the orthodox Roman Catholic view of justification is not a barrier to being one in Christ. It is clear that, by refusing to renounce ECT, they maintain

that unity in Christ does not require adherence
to the gospel of justification by faith alone.

Both Roman Catholic and professedly evangelical signatories of ECT acknowledged that
justification by faith alone is an acceptable formula, as is the Roman Catholic formula of justification by faith and works. One or the other
may be an individual's personal preference, but
that does not prevent recognizing as a brother
in Christ one who takes the alternative view.
The distinction between the gospel and the
Galatian heresy is thus placed on the same level
as the distinction between different millennial
views. So one has the most subtle form of
legalism to plague the church in its history.
While professing to believe the gospel, these
signers say rejection of the gospel, by replacing
it with the old Galatian variety of legalism, is
not a barrier to being one in Christ.

They might as well say, "If I or an angel
from heaven preach another gospel, let him be
acknowledged as my brother in Christ, co-
signer of religious manifestos, and co-author of
books encouraging ever greater degrees of coop-
eration." Paul, by the Spirit of God, condemns
those who collaborate with Galatian heretics as
well as the heretics themselves. By God's grace,
a growing number of Christian agencies and

institutions are exercising discipline by barring signatories of ECT from their ministries until these men repent and renounce the document by removing their names.

ECT has also produced one of the most extraordinary combinations of heresy in the history of the church. For arguably the first time in history, one can find persons who can legitimately be identified as both legalist and antinomian at the same time. Some of the professing evangelical writers have been long known for their antinomian writings. Their affirmation and defense of *Evangelicals and Catholics Together* has shown that they believe that holding to the legalistic Galatian heresy is not a barrier to being one in Christ. Although maintaining a personal theology which is antinomian, apparently at the same time they clearly believe that they can have spiritual unity with those persons who adhere to this variety of legalism. Either God has preserved these professing believers through unparalleled inconsistency while still maintaining in them a hidden love of the one true gospel, or consistently they are affirming a legalism that works → justification, one in which faith is the only work required. Thus one who has this humanly-produced faith is saved even if he erroneously

believes other man-made works are also prereq-
uisites, while from the signer's own perspective
faith is the only necessary work, not even
requiring subsequent good works as evidence of
true faith. The ECT document did not divide
evangelicalism; it merely revealed that many
professed evangelicals are as lost as orthodox
Roman Catholics.

Abuse of the Term "Legalism"
Before turning from the topic of legalism, it
is important to address the unfortunate abuse
of the term which has dominated contemporary
evangelical parlance. Safely 90 percent of the
time I have heard the term "legalism" used, it
has been abused. Rather than referring to the
doctrine that at least part of the gift of eternal
life is merited by my actions, "legalism" is used
to refer to an overly-heavy emphasis on certain
exegetically questionable (from the speaker's
perspective) ethical principles. A typical example of this abuse of the term would be, "I was
raised in a legalistic church that wouldn't let
anyone go to movies." This abuse of the term
both risks lessening the severity of just how
serious true legalism is and, on the other hand,
risks slandering evangelical brothers and sisters
who are defending the gospel. If the speaker

attacking the anti-movie church is able to show that in fact the church teaches that one is justified by faith and not going to movies, he has indeed proved that group to be a legalistic cult and not a church. This group would be analagous to the Judaizers of Galatians. If they met a professing believer who attended movies, they would tell him he cannot yet be a true believer because refraining from movies was a prerequisite to being a Christian. I hope I have shown how absurd—as well as uncharitable—this common use of the word is, and I doubt I have ever met a person throwing around that term loosely who, when confronted, felt he could establish such a claim.

As far as I can tell, the person who cries "legalism" is attacking groups who think the law of God requires explicitly or implicitly some action which he himself does not think is required. Going back to our example, it seems the response of the church members in question, if challenged on their position, would be that they believe that justification is by faith alone, and that part of the life of gratitude which flows out of being redeemed includes not attending movies. Obviously they are morally required to base their argument against movies on Scripture, and I am certain that they would be willing to take up that gauntlet. Whether they persuade others or not, these believers certainly are not legalists. The abuse of the term has distorted an exegetical question between two believers and made it seem to be a difference between the true and the false gospel! In the midst of the life-and-death struggle with true legalism, this ungracious and incorrect use of the term must stop.

One last word to those who believe the Word of God identifies a particular action as part of the path of grateful obedience for the converted while another professing believer does not. (I should note that this conflict is probably present in any pair of believers in some context or another.) In our example, the brother who thinks the Bible does not require him to refrain from going to movies may not be called an antinomian or libertine by the brother who does. Here too we have an exegetical difference between two believers, not a denial of the gospel. Part of growth in grace is being ever more able to see the implications of the Bible and not just the letter. As we who have walked in the Lord for years (and all who understand the Sermon on the Mount) know, the spirit of the law is more rigorous than the letter, not more lenient. Discipling a young Christian will inevitably help him see implications in the commandments of Christ which he had not originally seen, as it will also help him see where cultural values have been confused with implications of the law of God. However, that does not mean that one was claiming to be a believer while intentionally living in sin when he did not yet see the particular ramification of the law.

I have seen individuals go full circle in their spiritual life in this regard. First, as young Christians they kept an implicit command of God as they observed others in their church do it. Later, under influence of others who did not see the implication, they came to attack such practice incorrectly and unwisely as "legalistic." Finally, they discovered the biblical ground for the principle and were persuaded that the practice was in fact an implication of the law of God, and they returned to keeping it. Of course not all inferences are valid inferences, and some unconsciously allow cultural values to be confused with implications of Scripture, but we must not condemn even one who errs in drawing false inferences from the ethical teaching of Scripture as a legalist, nor one who fails to see the valid inferences of these teachings as an antinomian.

I trust this discussion has made all of us more interested in the field of practical biblical ethics, or, as the Puritans liked to call it, cases of conscience.

Classic Antinomianism: The Heresy of the Justified Pig

Dr. D. James Kennedy likes to illustrate the difference between sin in a believer's life and in an unbeliever's life by the analogy of the cat and the pig. If a cat falls in the mud, she immediately begins to clean herself off. If a pig falls in the mud, he gladly wallows in it, having found his own element. Antinomianism is the heresy of the justified pig:

Faith → Justification – Works

Antinomianism is also found in the heart of the visible church. It speaks eloquently of the need for saving faith in Christ. However, the faith spoken of is seen as not necessarily transforming the individual's life. "If you love Me, you will keep My commandments" (John 14:15) becomes a strange passage. The judgment on the last day including good deeds as the visible sign of true faith is also rejected despite abundant biblical evidence.

Scripture presents antinomianism as a satanic attack on the gospel. Reprobates slipped into the church, and these godless men "turn the grace of our God into an excuse for immorality" (Jude 4). Antinomianism is an anti-gospel every bit as surely as legalism. To say that a person can be transformed by the Spirit of God to believe the gospel and yet continue to live a life of immorality is an insult to the Spirit of God Himself.

The horrendous sins inflicted within the church by those claiming the name of Christ is appalling! A percentage of these outrages is likely the result of the failings of truly repentant saints, but Scripture explicitly states that many of these find their roots in wicked counterfeits who claim saving faith without the transformation which without exception flows from saving faith.

Let me use the seventh commandment as an illustration, given the epidemic of cases of sexual sin in professing evangelical circles. Please note this warning may be just as well applied to thieves or swindlers or slanderers; but no practicing adulterer will inherit the kingdom of God. Those who have been justified have by the power of the Holy Spirit put such deeds in the past tense. Often antinomians counter with the example of Christ's condemnation of lust as adultery of the heart. This is misinterpreted to

mean that any person who has an average
amount of sexual desire is in fact an adulterer.
In fact lust is also an overt sin, a choice to desire what one does not have. No believer will
practice lust any more than he will practice
adultery. Any practicing adulterer, one living in
explicit sexual immorality or the practice of
lust, will be lost eternally, be he a member of
the visible church or not.

One of the most beautiful historic statements of the gospel in rejection of antinomianism is to be found in the classic Lord's Supper
formula of the Dutch Reformed Church. It includes a long list of people who must not come
to the table of the Lord lest they make their
damnation more severe. In the list are many
explicit offenses, concluding with the summary
phrase, "all who lead offensive lives." It explains
this prohibition with remarkable biblical sim-
plicity. The table of the Lord is intended only
for believers. A true believer will not live in unrepentant sin. A person living in unrepentant
sin will not inherit the kingdom of God. Faith
yields justification; faith yields a changed life. A
believer may fall into sin, but he will not *live* in
sin. The formula makes clear that the remaining sin which is in us against our will (that is,
that which we are sincerely striving against)

cannot prevent us from being right partakers of the Lord's table, nor the wedding feast of the Lamb.

Classic antinomianism is founded in the deeply lost condition of man. Self-preservation and self-interest are attributes exhibited by all of God's creation. No one willingly chooses eternal suffering. (One would think this was self-evident, if not for the growing number of theologians who, in a desire to lessen the hellishness of hell, imply that the damned chose the option themselves.) But no spiritually dead person chooses to love God or his neighbor either. Antinomianism is the devilish doctrine that a believer can be saved *in* his sins, not *from* his sins. It claims that unrighteousness will inherit the kingdom of God.

Antinomians are cursed throughout the pages of Scripture. The sons of Eli were sons of Belial, yet still ministered in the church while living lives of unrepentant immorality. Most of the horrendous immorality which hides in the church then and now comes from these antinomians who are not merely antinomian in theology, but also in practice.

However, one finds a stranger problem than the active antinomian. This problem appears in those who themselves are not antinomian in their personal life, but defend antinomianism as a Christian possibility. These believers have a living faith, but call those with a dead faith brothers and sisters in Christ. Antinomianism is an option, albeit a road not recommended. It is the farthest-out lane of the narrow road, not the wrong turn off the edge that leads to the broad road. When they sing "Trust and obey for there is no other way to be *happy* in Jesus than to trust and obey," they presumably think that one may be *in* Jesus without trusting and obeying, but just not *happy* in Jesus. One may lose rewards in heaven, or peace of mind, or joy, but the bottom line for them remains that no pattern of lawlessness will disprove that one is a redeemed individual. As my father was fond of saying in response, "Trust and obey, for there's no other way to be *in* Jesus, not just happy!"

The Carnal Christian

A classic defense of antinomianism is the little tract produced by Bill Bright and his Campus Crusade movement known as "The Spirit-Filled Life." In it, the carnal Christian is presented as one who has accepted Christ into his heart as Savior, but not "let Him be Lord." Obviously the whole reason for the booklet is to encourage the carnal Christian to promote Christ to Lord. But indisputably the person who is currently rejecting Christ's Lordship, while claiming Him as Savior, is according to this tract still a saved Christian whether or not he heeds the advice.

Another classic is the booklet, "My House, Christ's Home." In it the individual accepts Christ into his life, and almost all of his life. But one room remains locked. Finally, years later, the door is opened and Christ is allowed in. So a converted person can hold onto the practice of a cherished sin, or maintain sovereignty over one part of his life for years, yet still be justified in God's eyes.

In fact, "no one who is born of God will continue to sin . . . he cannot go on sinning because he is born of God" (1 John 3:9). Christ is not in any house in which all doors are not opened. Certainly each believer finds certain sins to be special challenges, but he strives against all sins he is aware of, or he is not a believer.

The carnal Christian as discussed by Paul is by no means a person living in sin or denying Christ's Lordship. He is childishly viewing things from an earthly perspective and is not as discerning about spiritual realities as he ought to be. The carnal Christian has not grown up enough to know, for example, that it is sinful to elevate one teacher over another and therefore provoke schism in the church. This subtle sin is beyond his perception. He is not aware of that room in the basement, but he is not consciously barring Christ from it.

Theological Roots of Tolerance of Antinomianism

There are at least three factors which help to give birth to this strange hybrid among those who themselves evidence a living faith:

Pendulum Shift: One is an overreaction to legalism. The early church experienced a similar phenomenon. It staggered from heresy to heresy, first from a group claiming that Christ was God but not man, then that He was man but not God. So the antinomian struggles against legalism's "Faith + Works → Justification" by falling into the opposite error: Faith → Justification – Works. These thinkers sadly think they are defending the gospel against legalism, when in fact they are proclaiming another gospel.

Free from the Law: Secondly, dispensationalism has intentionally separated the old from the new covenant, viewing law as gospel. Freedom from the condemnation of the law through Christ came to be seen as freedom from the law as the principle of obedience written on the heart of true believers. Antinomianism is a natural consequence of failing to understand this unchanging role of the law throughout the history of the people of God.

Perseverance of the sinner: Finally, dispensationalism has tended to have a particularly confused sense of perseverance of the saints. Commonly called "once saved, always saved," this view substitutes a biblical focus on sanctification as the path of assurance with a once-for-all assurance given to anyone who believes, which no amount of sin can shake. Reformed biblical orthodoxy teaches that one who is truly redeemed will persevere and strive after righteousness until the end. One who remains in sin reveals himself to have not been truly justified.

Contemporary Twists on Antinomianism
The Sword Sheathers: Even those who reject antinomianism are in great danger of letting the gospel fruit of good works drop out of their own preaching. I have come to call this phenomenon of dulling the key teaching of the necessity of good works "sword-sheathing."

These teachers cheerfully tone down the passages which explicitly condemn antinomian
practice, and they thereby blunt the edge of the
Word. Their exposition of "No adulterer will
inherit the kingdom of God" leads to "So if you
are an adulterer, you *might not be* a Christian."
The literal word of God is softened to allow
antinomian practice in the kingdom.

Luther's False Friends: The great reformer
Martin Luther's vibrant defense of justification
by faith alone has been often misused by antinomians. At times it seems that Luther's every
idle word has been brought forth by antinomians. A balanced reading of Luther's theology
shows him to be an enemy of antinomianism.
Yet there are few figures in history easier to
twist by taking dramatic quotations out of
context.

Jesus Paid it All, Nothing to Him I Owe: A
surprisingly diverse group of professing
evangelicals has counseled rejection of the key
Christian concept of gratitude. This misunder-
standing usually comes from a failure to
distinguish Christ's complete redemption of all
who believe from our continuing debt to Him.
According to this false teaching, because Christ
has fully paid our debt we *must* do nothing.
"All my debt is paid." These antinomians end

that sentence with a period rather than a semi-colon. In the most extreme case, one is for-bidden even to confess one's sins, since Christ already paid them all!

In fact, all my debt is paid—even I myself have been purchased. Since we were bought with a price, all we have belongs to our Savior. Believers belong to Christ as slaves of righteousness (Romans 6:18) for His glory. The life of the believer is to confess our sins and strive daily against them, knowing that He is faithful and just to forgive us our sins and cleanse us from all unrighteousness (1 John 1:9). The clean disciples still needed the daily washing of their feet by Christ (John 13:10).

Some have more subtly doubted the value of gratitude as a motivation. The Scripture will have none of this. It is explicit about gratitude as motivation. "I love the Lord because He heard my voice" (Psalm 116:1). "If you love Me you will keep My commandments" (John 14:15). Because of Christ's grace, we are truly purchased for Him. We willingly live our lives full of gratitude for what our Master has done.

Antinomianism is a remarkably resilient heresy. It offers great happiness to the uncon-verted, and is frightfully tempting even to be-lievers. Yet no worker of iniquity will enter the kingdom of heaven. The redeemed will serve their Master with constant thankfulness for what He has done for them.

Back to Judgment Day

We have identified the chief theological errors of those who will run to Christ on that day calling Him "Lord," only to be rejected. Antinomians and legalists deny the Lord who, they claim, has bought them.

Any whose ground for claiming Christ as Savior is either a faith that does not produce a transformed life or a faith that is coupled with works as a necessary prerequisite to gaining eternal life will be lost eternally. Some who have preached the true gospel, and been used by the Spirit to lead others to eternal life, have in their own heart lived out another gospel with a dead, counterfeit faith. They will be lost, while some who heard the gospel from them will be saved.

To begin and end at judgment day has left the issue of legalism and antinomianism in the proper light. One question remains. We have said a person can preach the true gospel and be lost. Can one preach one of these false ways and be saved?

Part of the answer is painfully simple. If in their heart they are antinomian or legalist they are certainly condemned. If in their preaching they proclaim legalism or antinomianism as the gospel, they will certainly be doubly condemned. The agonizingly subtle question regards those who have falsely taught antinomianism and legalism as options for others, even though not recommended ones, while apparently having a living faith in the true gospel themselves.

Can one be saved and counsel another to travel peacefully on the broad road that leads to destruction? Obviously all professing evangelicals are appalled to hear of teachers who claim there are other ways to eternal life than the cross of Christ. Must we not be equally appalled to hear of teachers who say there are other ways of appropriating Christ than the gospel? We must reject any teacher who claims that there are other ways of salvation than by Christ, even if that teacher claims that he himself trusts in Christ. So we must reject any teacher *as* a teacher who claims that legalism or antinomianism in any form is acceptable, even though that person himself professes to follow the gospel.

God Himself determines the eternal destiny of all who teach in His name. However, I must, as a minister of the gospel, give a final warning

to any teachers who are defending the possibility of other ways of appropriating salvation
than by a living faith alone. The prophet
Ezekiel warns, regarding any who do not warn
the wicked to repent, that the blood of those
who perish will be upon their heads (Ezekiel
33). Paul reflects the eternal truth of that ad-
monition by declaring that he is innocent of the
blood of all men because he did not hold back
from declaring the whole counsel of God (Acts
20:22–23). An objective reading of Scripture
apart from looking at individuals would proclaim that no regenerate teacher will proclaim
or teach that heretical views of the gospel such
as antinomianism and legalism are permissible.
So no more will such a teacher, with the blood
of the lost on his head, inherit the kingdom
than an adulterer.

Judgment day is too serious a matter to
permit sheathing the sword on this issue. I can
express a personal hope that some such
teachers would be saved by fire if they were
sinning ignorantly when they taught such evil
options. But I also must say my personal hope
is conjecture; the Word's explicit statements
point in the opposite direction.

This chapter is being read by many pastors
living in unrepentant sin, including the unre-

pentant sin of declaring peace through another way than the true gospel. How I hope and pray that the Spirit will convict all who read this in such a state to repent and believe the good news. May that day dawn when we can run to meet our Lord in appropriate joy, being clothed in His righteousness which we received by a living faith that led us constantly to strive against sin, especially the sin of encouraging other gospels. What an inexpressible joy to be able to hear those precious words, "Abide with Me, I *always* knew you."

Glad Obedience
(The Third Use of the Law)

Joel Beeke and Ray Lanning

Keep me from falsehood, let Thy law
With me in grace abide;
The way of faithfulness I choose,
Thy precepts are my guide.

I cleave unto Thy truth, O Lord;
From shame deliver me;
In glad obedience I will live
Through strength bestowed by Thee.[1]

The law of God addresses the world and the life of every individual directly or indirectly. Protestant theologians have written much about the various applications or uses of the law in the life of society at large and in the individual lives of both the unbeliever and the Christian. Classic Protestant theology posits a threefold use of the law: the *usus primus* ("first use"), or *civil* use of the law in the life and affairs of state and society; the *usus secundus* ("second use"), or *evangelical* use of the law as a teacher of sin in the experience or process of conversion unto God; and the *usus tertius* ("third use"), or *didactic* use of the law as a rule of thankful obedience on the part of the Christian.[2] It is this last or third use of the law that inspired the prayer of the psalmist cited above, for he knows that only God's law can direct him as he endeavors to live "in glad obedience" as a child of God.

The Uses of the Law

In this chapter we briefly summarize the first two uses of the law in order to examine its third use in the proper context of sanctification, which necessarily involves grateful obedience to God for His full-orbed salvation in Jesus Christ. The believer who is justified by faith alone (*sola fide*), and who adheres to the principle of "Scripture alone" (*sola scriptura*), will thankfully and wholeheartedly trust and obey the Lord. This response of grateful obedience is fleshed out in a case study of the law's most controversial commandment: keeping the Sabbath day holy. All of this enables us to draw several significant conclusions about the Christian in his relationship to the third use of the law.

The Civil Use of the Law

The first use of the law is its function in

public life as a guide to the civil magistrate in his task as the minister of God in things pertaining to the state. The magistrate is required to reward good and punish evil (Romans 13:3–4). Nothing could be more essential to this work than a reliable standard of right and wrong, good and evil; and no better standard can be found than the law of God.

Here the Protestant Reformers were in complete accord. Concerning the restraint of sin, Martin Luther writes in his *Lectures on Galatians* (3:19), "The first understanding and use of the law is to restrain the wicked. . . . This civic restraint is extremely necessary and was instituted by God, both for the sake of public peace and for the sake of preserving everything, but especially to prevent the course of the gospel from being hindered by the tumults and seditions of wild men."[3]

John Calvin concurs:

> The . . . function of the law is this: at least by fear of punishment to restrain certain men who are untouched by any care for what is just and right unless compelled by hearing the dire threats in the law. But they are restrained not because their inner mind is stirred or affected, but because, being bridled, so to speak, they keep their

> hands from outward activity, and hold
> inside the depravity that otherwise they
> would wantonly have indulged.[4]

The civil use of the law is rooted thoroughly in the Scriptures (most specifically in Romans 13:1–7) and in a realistic doctrine of fallen human nature. The law teaches us that the powers that be are ordained of God in order to administer justice—justice which necessarily includes being a terror to the workers of iniquity. The powers that be bear the sword; they possess a divinely conferred right of punishment, even of ultimate capital punishment (verses 3–4).

This first use of the law, however, serves not only to prevent society from lapsing into chaos; it also serves to promote righteousness: "I exhort therefore, that, first of all, supplications, prayers, intercessions, and giving of thanks, be made for all men, for kings and for all that are in authority; that we may lead a quiet and peaceable life in all godliness and honesty" (1 Timothy 2:1–2). The "higher powers" must strive not only to intimidate evil, but also to provide a peaceable context in which the gospel, godliness, and honesty may prosper. This duty compels the state, the Reformers believed, to preserve certain rights such as freedom of worship, freedom to preach, and freedom to observe the Lord's Day.

The implications of the first use of the law for the Christian are inescapable: He must respect and obey the state so long as the state does not command what God forbids or forbid what God commands. In all other cases, civil disobedience is unlawful. To resist authority is to resist the ordinance of God, "and they that resist shall receive to themselves damnation" (Romans 13:2). This is critical to affirm in our day when even Christians are prone to be swept along with a worldly spirit of rebellion and contempt for authority. We need to hear and heed what Calvin writes:

> The first duty of subjects toward their magistrates is to think most honorably of their office, which they recognize as a jurisdiction bestowed by God, and on that account to esteem and reverence them as ministers and representatives of God. . . . [Even] in a very wicked man utterly unworthy of all honor, provided he has the public power in his hands, that noble and divine power resides which the Lord has by his Word given to the ministers of his justice and judgment.[5]

Of course, this does not imply that the believer forfeits his right to criticize or even con-

demn legislation which strays from the principles of Scripture. It does mean that a significant
part of our "adorning the doctrine of God"
(Titus 2:10) involves our willing subjection to
lawful authority in every sphere of life—be it in
the home, school, church, or state.

The Evangelical Use of the Law[6]

Wielded by the Spirit of God, the moral law
also serves a critical function in the experience
of conversion. It disciplines, educates, convicts,
and curses. The law not only exposes our sinfulness; it also condemns us, pronounces a
curse upon us, and declares us liable to the
wrath of God and the torments of hell. "Cursed
is every one that continueth not in all things
which are written in the book of the law to do
them" (Galatians 3:10). The law is a hard taskmaster; it knows no mercy. It terrifies us,
strips us of all our righteousness, and drives us
to the end of the law, Christ Jesus, who is our
only acceptable righteousness with God.
"Wherefore the law was our schoolmaster to
bring us unto Christ, that we might be justified
by faith" (Galatians 3:24). Not that the law itself can lead us to a saving knowledge of God in
Christ. Rather, the Holy Spirit uses the law as a
mirror to show us our impotence and our guilt,

to shut us up to hope in mercy alone, and to induce repentance, creating and sustaining the sense of spiritual need out of which faith in Christ is born.

Here, too, Luther and Calvin see eye to eye.[7] Typical of Luther's writings are his comments on Galatians 2:17:

> The proper use and aim of the Law is to make guilty those who are smug and at peace, so that they may see that they are in danger of sin, wrath, and death, so that they may be terrified and despairing, blanching and quaking at the rustling of a leaf (Leviticus 26:36). . . . If the Law is a ministry of sin, it follows that it is also a ministry of wrath and death. For just as the Law reveals sin, so it strikes the wrath of God into a man and threatens him with death.[8]

Calvin is no less intense:

> [The law] warns, informs, convicts, and lastly condemns, every man of his own unrighteousness. . . . After he is compelled to weigh his life in the scales of the law, laying aside all that presumption of fictitious righteousness, he discovers that he is a long way from holiness, and is in

> fact teeming with a multitude of vices,
> with which he previously thought him-
> self undefiled. . . . The law is like a mirror.
> In it we contemplate our weakness, then
> the iniquity arising from this, and finally
> the curse coming from both—just as a
> mirror shows us the spots on our face.[9]

This convicting use of the law is also critical for the believer's sanctification, for it serves to prevent the resurrection of self-righteousness— that ungodly self-righteousness which is always prone to reassert itself even in the holiest of saints. The believer continues to live under the law as a lifelong penitent.

This chastening work of the law does not imply that the believer's justification is ever diminished or annulled. From the moment of regeneration, his state before God is fixed and irrevocable. He is a new creation in Christ Jesus (2 Corinthians 5:17). He can never revert to a state of condemnation nor lose his sonship. Nevertheless, the law exposes the ongoing poverty of his sanctification on a daily basis. He learns that there is a law in his members such that, when he would do good, evil is present with him (Romans 7:21). He must repeatedly condemn himself, deplore his wretchedness, and cry daily for fresh applications of the blood

of Jesus Christ that cleanses from all sin
(Romans 7:24; 1 John 1:7, 9).

The Didactic Use of the Law

The third or didactic use of the law addresses the daily life of the Christian. In the
words of the Heidelberg Catechism, the law instructs the believer how to express gratitude to
God for deliverance from all his sin and misery
(Q. 2). The third use of the law is a subject that
fills a rich chapter in the history of Reformation doctrine.

Philip Melanchthon (1497-1560). The history
of the third use of the law begins with Philip
Melanchthon, Martin Luther's co-worker and
right-hand support. Already, in 1521, Melanchthon had planted the seed when he affirmed
that "believers have use of the Decalogue" to
assist them in mortifying the flesh.[10] In a for-
mal sense he increased the number of functions
or uses of the law from two to three for the first
time in a third edition of his work on Colossians published in 1534[11]—two years before
Calvin produced the first edition of his
Institutes. Melanchthon argued that the law co-
erces (first use), terrifies (second use), and requires obedience (third use). "The third reason
for retaining the Decalogue," he writes, "is that

obedience is required."[12]

By 1534 Melanchthon was using the forensic nature of justification as bedrock for establishing the necessity of good works in the believer's life.[13] He argued that though the believer's first and primary righteousness was his justification in Christ, there was also a second righteousness—the righteousness of a good conscience which, notwithstanding its imperfection, is still pleasing to God since the believer himself is in Christ.[14] The conscience of the believer, made good by divine declaration, must continue to use the law to please God, for the law reveals the essence of God's will and provides the framework of Christian obedience. He asserted that this "good conscience" is a "great and necessary godly consolation."[15] As Timothy Wengert asserts, he was no doubt encouraged to emphasize the connection between a good conscience and good works by his desire to defend Luther and other Protestants from the charge that they deny good works "without at the same time robbing the conscience of the gospel's consolation. He thus devised a way to speak of the necessity of works for the believer by excluding their necessity for justification."[16] Wengert concludes that, by arguing from the necessity of knowing how we are forgiven to the

necessity of obeying the law and to the necessity of knowing how this obedience pleases
God, Melanchthon managed to place law and
obedience at the center of his theology.[17]

Martin Luther (1483–1546). Unlike Melanchthon, who went on to codify the third use of
the law in the 1535 and 1555 editions of his
major work on Christian doctrine,[18] Luther
never saw a need to embrace formally a third
use of the law. Lutheran scholars, however, have
debated at length whether Luther actually
taught in fact, though not in name, a third use
of the law.[19] Suffice it to say that Luther advo-
cated that though the Christian is not "under
the law," this ought not be understood as if he
were "without the law." For Luther, the believer
has a different attitude toward the law. The law
is not an obligation, but a delight. He is joyfully
moved towards God's law by the Spirit's power.
He conforms to the law freely, not because of
the law's demands, but because of his love for
God and His righteousness.[20] Since in his experience the law's heavy yoke is replaced by the
light yoke of Christ, doing what the law commands becomes a joyous and spontaneous action. The law drives sinners to Christ through
whom they "become doers of the law."[21] Moreover, because he remains sinful, the Christian

needs the law to direct and regulate his life. Thus Luther can assert that the law, which serves as a "stick" (i.e., rod—second use) God uses to beat him to Christ, is simultaneously a "stick" (i.e., cane—which Calvin would call the third use) that assists him in walking the Christian life. This emphasis on the law as a "walking-stick" is borne out implicitly by his exposition of the Ten Commandments in various contexts—each of which indicates that he firmly believed that the Christian life is to be regulated by these commandments.[22]

Luther's concern was not to deny sanctification or the law as a guiding norm in the believer's life; rather, he wished to emphasize that good works and obedience to the law can in no way make us acceptable with God. Hence he writes in *The Freedom of the Christian,* "Our faith in Christ does not free us from works, but from false opinions concerning works, that is, from the foolish presumption that justification is acquired by works." And in *Table Talk* he is quoted as saying, "Whoso has Christ has rightly fulfilled the law, but to take away the law altogether, which sticks in nature, and is written in our hearts and born in us, is a thing impossible and against God."[23]

John Calvin (1509–1559). What Melanchthon

began to develop in the direction of a God-pleasing righteousness in Christ, and what Luther left somewhat undeveloped as a joyous action and a "walking-stick," Calvin fleshed out as a full-fledged doctrine, teaching that the primary use of the law for the believer is as a rule of life. Though Calvin borrowed Melanchthon's term, "third use of the law" (*tertius usus legis*) and probably gleaned additional material from Martin Bucer,[24] he provided new contours and content to the doctrine and was unique among the early Reformers in stressing that this third function of the law, as a norm and guide for the believer, is its "proper and principal" use.[25]

Calvin's teaching on the third use of the law is crystal clear. "What is the rule of life which [God] has given us?" he asks in the Genevan Catechism, and replies, "His law." Later in the same catechism, he writes:

> [The law] shows the mark at which we ought to aim, the goal towards which we ought to press, that each of us, according to the measure of grace bestowed upon him, may endeavour to frame his life according to the highest rectitude, and, by constant study, continually advance more and more.[26]

Calvin wrote definitively of the third use of
the law as early as 1536 in the first edition of
his *Institutes of the Christian Religion:*

> Believers . . . profit by the law because
> from it they learn more thoroughly each
> day what the Lord's will is like. . . . It is as
> if some servant, already prepared with
> complete earnestness of heart to com-
> mend himself to his master, must search
> out and oversee his master's ways in or-
> der to conform and accommodate himself
> to them. Moreover, however much they
> may be prompted by the Spirit and eager
> to obey God, they are still weak in the
> flesh, and would rather serve sin than
> God. The law is to this flesh like a whip to
> an idle and balky ass, to goad, stir, arouse
> it to work.[27]

In the last edition of the *Institutes,* completed in 1559, Calvin retains what he wrote in
1536, but stresses even more clearly and positively that believers profit from the law in two
ways: first, "here is the best instrument for
them to learn more thoroughly each day the
nature of the Lord's will to which they aspire,
and to confirm them in the understanding of
it"; second, by "frequent meditation upon it to
be aroused to obedience, be strengthened in it,

and be drawn back from the slippery path of transgression. In this way the saints must press on." Calvin concludes: "For what would be less lovable than the law if, with importuning and threatening alone, it troubled souls through fear, and distressed them through fright? David especially shows that in the law he apprehended the Mediator, without whom there is no delight or sweetness."[28]

This predominantly positive view of the law as a norm and guide for the believer, to encourage him to cling to God and to obey God ever more fervently, is where Calvin distances himself from Luther. For Luther, the law generally denotes something negative and hostile—something usually listed in close proximity with sin, death, or the devil. Luther's dominant interest is in the second use of the law, even when he considers the function of the law in sanctifying the believer. For Calvin, as I. John Hesselink correctly notes, "the law was viewed primarily as a positive expression of the will of God. . . . Calvin's view could be called Deuteronomic, for to him law and love are not antithetical, but are correlates."[29] For Calvin, the believer strives to follow God's law not as an act of *compulsory* obedience, but as a response of *grateful* obedience. The law promotes, under the tutelage of

the Spirit, an ethic of gratitude in the believer,
which both encourages loving obedience and
cautions him against sin, so that he sings with
David in Psalm 19:

> *Most perfect is the law of God,*
> *Restoring those that stray;*
> *His testimony is most sure,*
> *Proclaiming wisdom's way.*
>
> *The precepts of the Lord are right;*
> *With joy they fill the heart;*
> *The Lord's commandments all are pure,*
> *And clearest light impart.*
>
> *The fear of God is undefiled*
> *And ever shall endure;*
> *The statutes of the Lord are truth*
> *And righteousness most pure.*
>
> *They warn from ways of wickedness*
> *Displeasing to the Lord,*
> *And in the keeping of His word*
> *There is a great reward.*[30]

In sum, for Luther, the law *helps* the believer—especially in recognizing and con-
fronting indwelling sin; for Calvin, the believer

needs the law to direct him in holy living in order to serve God out of love.[31]

The Heidelberg Catechism (1563). Ultimately, Calvin's view of the third use of the law won the day in Reformed theology. An early indication of this strongly Calvinistic view of the law is found in the Heidelberg Catechism, composed a year or two before Calvin's death. Though the Catechism begins with an intense emphasis on the evangelical use of the law in driving sinners to Christ (Questions 3–18), a detailed exhortation on the prohibitions and requirements of the law placed upon the believer is reserved for the final section which teaches "how I shall express my *gratitude* to God" for deliverance in Jesus Christ (Questions 92–115).[32] The Decalogue provides the material content for good works which are done out of thankfulness for the grace of God in His beloved Son.

The Puritans. The Puritans carried on Calvin's emphasis on the normativity of the law for the believer as a rule of life and to arouse heartfelt gratitude, which in turn promotes genuine liberty rather than antinomian licentiousness.[33] To cite only a few of hundreds of Puritan sources available on these themes: Anthony Burgess condemns those who assert that they are above the law or that the law written in the heart by regeneration "renders the written law needless."[34] Typically Puritan is Thomas Bedford's affirmation of the need for the written law as the believer's guide:

> There must also be another law written in tables, and to be read by the eye, to be heard by the ear: Else . . . how shall the believer himself be sure that he doth not swerve from the right way wherein he ought to walk? . . . The Spirit, I grant, is the justified man's Guide and Teacher. . . . But he teacheth them . . . by the law and testimony.[35]

The Spirit's teaching results in Christians being made "friends" with the law, Samuel Rutherford quipped, for "after Christ has made agreement between us and the law, we delight to walk in it for the love of Christ."[36] That delight, grounded in gratitude for the gospel, produces an unspeakable liberty. Samuel Crooke put it this way: "From the commandment, as a rule of life, [believers] are not freed, but on the contrary, are inclined and disposed, by [their] free spirit, to willingly obey it. Thus to the regenerate the law becomes as it were gospel, even a law of liberty."[37] The Westminster Larger Catechism, which was composed largely by Puritan divines, provides the most fitting summary of the Reformed and Puritan view on the believer's relationship to the moral law:

> Q. 97. What special use is there of the moral law to the regenerate?
> A. Although they that are regenerate, and believe in Christ, be delivered from the moral law as a covenant of works, so as thereby they are neither justified nor condemned; yet, besides the general uses thereof common to them with all men, it is of special use, to shew them how much they are bound to Christ for His fulfilling it, and enduring the curse thereof in their stead, and for their good; and thereby to provoke them to more thankfulness, and to express the same in their greater care to conform themselves thereunto as the rule of their obedience.[38]

But how do the Reformation principles of gratitude work themselves out in actual practice as the believer seeks to obey the law as a rule of life? To this question we now turn in the form of a case study as we consider the moral law's most controversial commandment in our day: "Remember the sabbath day, to keep it holy" (Exodus 20:8).

The Fourth Commandment: A Case Study

Central to the concern fostered by Reformed Christianity to apply the moral law to Christian living has been the sanctification of the first day of the week as the Christian Sabbath. If there was any degree of ambiguity among the Protestant Reformers of the sixteenth century, it had utterly vanished when, in the middle of the seventeenth century, the Westminster divines assembled to write their Confession of Faith (Chapter 21):

> 7. As it is the law of nature, that, in general, a due proportion of time be set apart for the worship of God; so, in His Word, by a positive, moral, and perpetual commandment, binding all men, in all ages, He hath particularly appointed one day in seven, for a Sabbath, to be kept holy unto Him: which, from the beginning of the world to the resurrection of Christ, was the last day of the week; and, from the resurrection of Christ, was changed into the first day of the week, which, in Scripture, is called the Lord's Day, and is to be continued to the end of the world, as the Christian Sabbath.
>
> 8. This Sabbath is then kept holy unto the Lord when men, after a due preparing of their hearts, and ordering of their common affairs beforehand, do not only ob-

> serve an holy rest, all the day, from their
> own works, words, and thoughts about
> their worldly employments, and recre-
> ations, but also are taken up the whole
> time in the public and private exercises of
> His worship, and in the duties of neces-
> sity and mercy.[39]

This high view of the Sabbath won the day in
Britain, North America, throughout the British
Empire, and also in the Netherlands. Though it
was a key concern of the Reformed Christians,
Sabbath observance was embraced as a rule by
Christians of nearly every denomination. In the
wake of the powerful revivals of the mid-
eighteenth and early nineteenth centuries,
Sabbath-keeping was embraced by the general
population as well.

This happy state of affairs prevailed
throughout the last century and into our own.
Large urban centers such as Philadelphia and
Toronto were known for the care with which
the Sabbath was observed by their inhabitants.
Down to the end of the last century, some major railroads ceased operations on Sundays.
Seaside resorts took such measures as banning
all motor traffic from the streets on Sundays
(Ocean Grove, N.J.) and the use of movie
houses for public worship on Sunday evenings

(Ocean City, N.J.).

Today's culture presents a vastly altered scene. The forces of secularization and the rise of the leisure culture, obsessed with pursuing recreations of all kinds, have extinguished concern for Sabbath observance in the general population. Even more tragic is the steady erosion of conviction on the part of Christians. The greatest damage was done by modernism's attack on the authority of Scripture, thus undermining and overthrowing all biblical norms for living. However, fundamentalism must also bear its share of the blame. Under the influence of dispensationalism, a growing antinomianism developed in the most conservative circles of American Christians. The Old Testament in general, and the moral law in particular, came to be regarded as monuments of a bygone era. The result has been wholesale destruction of conviction regarding the Sabbath, even among Presbyterians who subscribe to the Westminster Standards—notwithstanding the jarring inconsistency involved!

Surely the time is ripe for Christians to look once more to God's Word for instruction regarding the Fourth Commandment and its claims upon us. If for no other reason, the study should be undertaken in view of the mounting evidence of the high degree of destructive stress lurking behind the appealing facade of the so-called "culture of leisure." Men are destroying themselves because they cannot say no, whether at work or at play. Great spiritual blessings are promised to those who subject themselves to the self-denying discipline of Sabbath observance.

The Sabbath as a Divine Institution
"The seventh day is the sabbath of the LORD thy God" (Exodus 20:10). These words remind us that the Sabbath is a divine institution in two senses. First, the weekly Sabbath is instituted by God's word of command. Second, God claims the day as His own: "the sabbath of Jehovah thy God." The six days of the work week are ceded to man for his labor and leisure pursuits; not so the Sabbath, which God names as "my holy day" in Isaiah 58:13. Not to devote the day to the purposes and activities commanded for its sanctification is to rob God of that which belongs to Him.

This truth is reinforced by the words of the Lord Jesus Christ recorded by the first three evangelists (Matthew 12:8, Mark 2:28, and Luke 6:5) when He said, "The Son of man is Lord of the sabbath." At one blow, Christ asserts His

full deity and identity with Jehovah and reaf-
firms the claim of God upon the hours of the
weekly Sabbath, embracing the claim and re-
stating it in His own name. The claim left its
mark on the beliefs, practices, and usages of the
apostolic church, so that, by the end of that era,
the Christian Sabbath was known as "the Lord's
day" (Revelation 1:10).

The Sabbath as a Creation Ordinance

A common error is to assume that the
Sabbath originates with the giving of the law at
Sinai. Such a view ignores the fact that the Sabbath is not introduced as something new, but
rather acknowledged as something ancient and
historic that is now to be recalled and observed
by God's people: "*Remember* the sabbath day, to
keep it holy" (Exodus 20:8).

And what, specifically, is to be remembered
in the pattern of six days of work punctuated
by a day of holy rest? "In six days the LORD
made heaven and earth, the sea, and all that in
them is, and rested the seventh day: wherefore
the LORD blessed the sabbath day, and hal-
lowed it" (Exodus 20:11).

The biblical answer to the question of when
the Sabbath was instituted, and by whom, is
abundantly clear: the Sabbath was instituted by

God at the very dawn of history. Of course, man was present, and significantly, it was the first full day of his life on earth (Genesis 2:1–3). Whether the pattern was perpetuated after that point or not is perhaps a matter of speculation, but the history of the Sabbath was not lost. All that was necessary at Sinai was to recall that history, and to charge the people to keep up the remembrance of it ever afterwards.

The Sabbath is therefore not strictly a Mosaic ordinance. Its origin is rooted in creation itself, and, like marriage, the Sabbath is an institution of the highest significance to the human race. Its temporal blessings may be enjoyed by all mankind, and its spiritual blessings are promised to all who seek them, even to the "eunuchs" and "the sons of the stranger, that join themselves to the LORD" (Isaiah 56:1–8).

The Sabbath as a Redemptive Memorial
In the recapitulation of the Ten Commandments (Deuteronomy 5:6–21), we discover that redemption does not alter or annul the requirement to keep the Sabbath holy. Rather, it only adds to the meaning of the day for those who are "the redeemed of the LORD." Just as in the New Testament slaves were to share fully

with their masters in the blessing of the gospel, so it was a law in Israel that servants were to enjoy the rest provided for in the Fourth Commandment along with their masters: "that thy manservant and thy maidservant may rest as well as thou" (Deuteronomy 5:14). To this is added the following reminder: "And remember that thou wast a servant in the land of Egypt, and that the LORD thy God brought thee out thence through a mighty hand and by a stretched out arm: therefore the LORD thy God commanded thee to keep the sabbath day" (v. 15). With these words the Sabbath assumes a new meaning and function as a memorial of the redemption from bondage which God wrought for His people. This added meaning reinforces the Sabbath as an institution among God's people.

Here also is an anticipation of the impact of Christ's death and resurrection on the Sabbath observance of His followers. So great was this climactic and decisive fulfillment of the promise of redemption, closely followed by the outpouring of the Spirit on the day of Pentecost, that from that time onward the Sabbath "was changed into the first day of the week, which, in Scripture, is called the Lord's Day, and is to be continued to the end of the world, as the

Christian Sabbath" (Westminster Confession of Faith, XXI:7).

The result is that, as the apostle Paul writes in Hebrews 4:9, "There remaineth therefore a rest to the people of God." The Sabbath is with us still as a sign of something that is yet to be attained, experienced, and enjoyed in the eternal state. At the same time, because the word he uses for "rest" is *sabbatismos*, or "a keeping of a sabbath" (see KJV margin), the obligation to observe a weekly Sabbath continues under the gospel. Sabbath-keeping became in fact a mark of Christian discipleship in the age of the martyrs, as Maurice Roberts relates:

> One question put to the martyrs before they were put to death was: "*Dominicum servasti?*" (Do you keep the Lord's Day?)[40]

The Sabbath as Eschatological Sign
The prophecy of Isaiah closes with the announcement of the promise of the new heavens and the new earth for God's people: "For, behold, I create new heavens and a new earth: and the former shall not be remembered, nor come into mind" (Isaiah 65:17). In this new creation, the labor of God's people shall be wholly redeemed from the curse: "They shall not labor in vain, nor bring forth trouble, for they are the

seed of the blessed of the LORD, and their offspring with them" (v. 23).

This new order of creation will abide as the
consummation of the promise of redemption.
Not only is the labor of God's people to be
wholly redeemed from the curse; the Sabbath
also will at last come into its own as the universal day for the worship of Jehovah. Such is the
promise of God:

> For as the new heavens and the new
> earth, which I will make, shall remain be-
> fore Me, saith the LORD, so shall your
> seed and your name remain. And it shall
> come to pass, that from one new moon to
> another, and from one sabbath to another,
> shall all flesh come to worship before Me,
> saith the LORD (Isaiah 66:22–23).

To sum up, the Sabbath stands as an institution as old as creation itself. It belongs to the
order of things as they were at the beginning,
before man's fall into sin. It is as universal as
any other creation ordinance, holding the
promise of blessing for all mankind. The
promise of redemption and its fulfillment only
add to the significance of the Sabbath as a day
to be observed by the redeemed of the Lord.
The Sabbath is a sign of the promise of redemption, both in its fulfillment now, and also

in that which is yet to be. It is God's day, a
holy day—a day for Christians to keep holy.

Christ and the Sabbath
The Sabbath is as much a feature of the New
Testament landscape as of the Old. The question of the Sabbath and how it ought to be kept
was an oft-revisited battlefield in Christ's conflicts with the Pharisees. So intense was His
opposition to the Pharisees' ideas of Sabbath-
keeping that many have concluded that Christ
was opposed to the Sabbath itself, and would
therefore be opposed to any continuation of
Sabbath-keeping among His followers.

Such a conclusion ignores or conflicts with
three key facts of the gospel records. First,
Christ Himself kept the Sabbath faithfully (see
Luke 4:16). Second, Christ declared that He had
not come to destroy the law, and it follows
therefore that He had not come to destroy or
abolish the Sabbath (see Matthew 5:17). Third,
Christ claimed the Sabbath as His own, as we
have seen already: "The Son of man is Lord of
the sabbath."

Christ's conflict with the Pharisees must be
viewed therefore as a campaign not to destroy,
but rather to reclaim and restore the biblical institution of the Sabbath. Accordingly Christ

embraced the Sabbath and claimed it as His own. Moreover, He declared that He personally will fulfill the promise of the Sabbath in the lives of His disciples: "Come unto Me, all ye that labor and are heavy laden, and I will give you rest. Take My yoke upon you, and learn of Me; for I am meek and lowly in heart: and ye shall find rest unto your souls" (Matthew 11:28–29). Even here Christ sounds the note of opposition to the Pharisees and their "yoke" of traditional proscriptions and prohibitions regarding the Sabbath. Peter referred to this yoke, and declared it was one "neither our fathers nor we were able to bear" (Acts 15:10). Christ offers a very different yoke and says, "My yoke is easy, and My burden is light" (Matthew 11:30). To take Christ's yoke is to become His disciple, just as to take that of the Pharisees was to become theirs. To those who embrace Christ with a true faith, He promises rest as the fulfillment of redemption, in sharp contrast to the denial of that rest to the unbelieving and disobedient Israelites (Psalm 95:10–11). This rest consists of putting an end to the fruitless toil of seeking to be justified by works of the law. Christ also lifts from our backs the burden of the guilt of all our sins. Nor is this all, for there is the promise of more to come when we have put off "this body of death" (Romans 7:25, margin):

> And I heard a voice from heaven saying
> unto me, Write, Blessed are the dead
> which die in the Lord from henceforth:
> Yea, saith the Spirit, that they may rest
> from their labors; and their works do fol-
> low them (Revelation 14:13)

With this in mind, the apostle reminds believers of "a promise being left us of entering
into His rest," and adds this exhortation, in-
volving a profound play on words: "Let us labor
therefore to enter into that rest" (Hebrews 4:1,
11).

The Christian and the Sabbath

How should the followers of Christ keep the
Sabbath today? Many writers have offered answers to this question.[41] For the present purpose, however, we prefer to point to three rich
sources of guidance: the Fourth Commandment
itself; the prophet Isaiah; and the teachings and
example of Christ Jesus our Lord.

The Fourth Commandment in its two
canonical forms (Exodus 20:8–11 and Deuteronomy 5:12–15) provides much instruction.
First, we must lay aside our daily tasks and
employments. We must do so individually, as

families, as congregations, and as communities. Second, we must turn our minds and hearts to the great themes of Holy Scripture: the wonderful works of God as Creator, Redeemer, and Sanctifier. Third, we must engage in those activities which obtain, increase, and express knowledge of the holiness of God, and our own holiness in Christ. "Remember the sabbath day, to keep it *holy*."

The prophet Isaiah lived in a day much like our own, a time of prosperity and general affluence. He has a clear word to say about the perils of such affluence, in the form of the "culture of leisure" that prosperity makes possible:

> If thou turn away thy foot from the sabbath, from doing thy pleasure on My holy day; and call the sabbath a delight, the holy of the LORD, honourable; and shalt honour Him, not doing thine own ways, nor finding thine own pleasure, nor speaking thine own words: then shalt thou delight thyself in the LORD; and I will cause thee to ride upon the high places of the earth, and feed thee with the heritage of Jacob thy father: for the mouth of the LORD hath spoken it" (Isaiah 58:13–14).

Here the prophet extends the ban on engag-

ing in labor to include the pursuit of our personal recreations and leisure-time activities.
Even the words we speak are to be regulated by
the commandment. In return, the prophet
promises a wonderful kind of spiritual liberty
and enjoyment of God: "Then shalt thou delight thyself in the LORD!"

Finally, we must consider the teachings and
example of the Lord Jesus Christ. He stamped
the day with an indelible Christian character
when He said, "The Son of man is Lord of the
sabbath day." Henceforth it was only right to
speak of the *Christian* Sabbath. He reclaimed
the day as an institution designed for the good
and blessing of mankind when he reminded the
Pharisees that "the sabbath was made for man,
and not man for the sabbath" (Mark 2:27). He
taught us thereby not to encumber the day
with strictures that work against basic human
needs. He further insisted that "it is lawful . . .
to do well" (Matthew 12:12) and "lawful to do
good" (Luke 6:9) on the sabbath days. Here He
sanctions works of mercy and compassion done
in His name and for His sake.

From Christ's example we learn diligently
to attend the church of God, assembling on the
Sabbath to hear God's Word (Luke 4:16). It is
likewise a day on which the ministers of the

Word are to devote themselves to teaching and preaching (Luke 4:31). It is a day to do good to our fellow members of the household of faith (Luke 4:38–39) and to extend and receive the grace of Christian hospitality (Luke 14:1) as part of the fellowship of the saints appropriate to the day (see also Luke 24:29, 42). Finally, the Sabbath days are to be the great days for the manifestation and enjoyment of the grace of God revealed in the gospel—grace that opens our blind eyes, rebukes in us the fever of sin, sets us free from our sore bondage, triumphs over the devil and his host, restores what sin has caused to wither away, and heals all the sicknesses of our hearts and minds. It can fairly be said that everything Christ ever did on the Sabbath was aimed at this one thing, to reveal and proclaim the grace of God to sinners.

We conclude therefore that to omit or neglect the sanctification of the Christian Sabbath is to disobey God, break faith with the Lord Jesus, and rob ourselves of great blessing. Likewise, to keep the Sabbath as it ought to be kept, according to the teaching and example of our Lord, is a large part of living to the glory of God, and is nothing less than "to begin in this life the eternal sabbath" (Heidelberg Catechism, Q. 103).

Conclusions

Biblical Character of the Third Use of the Law

Several important conclusions about the Christian's third use of the law can now be drawn.[42] First, the third use of the law is *biblical*. Old and New Testament scriptures teem with expositions of the law directed primarily at believers to assist them in the abiding pursuit of sanctification. The Psalms repeatedly affirm that the believer relishes the law of God both in the inner man and in his outward life.[43] One of the psalmists' greatest concerns is to ascertain the good and perfect will of God, and then to run in the way of His commandments. The Sermon on the Mount and the ethical portions of Paul's epistles are prime New Testament examples of the law being used as a rule of life. The directions contained in these portions of Scripture are intended primarily for those already redeemed, and seek to encourage them to reflect a theology of grace with an ethics of gratitude. In this ethics of gratitude the believer lives out of and follows in the footsteps of his Savior, who was Himself the Servant of the Lord and Law-Fulfiller, daily obeying all His Father's commandments throughout His earthly sojourn.

Contrary to Antinomianism and Legalism

Second, the third use of the law combats both *antinomianism* and *legalism*. Antinomianism (*anti*=against; *nomos*=law) teaches that Christians no longer have any obligation toward the moral law because Jesus has fulfilled it and freed them from it in saving them by grace alone. Paul, of course, strongly rejected this heresy in Romans 3:8, as did Luther in his battles against Johann Agricola, and as did the New England Puritans in their opposition to Anne Hutchinson. Antinominians misunderstand the nature of justification by faith, which, though granted apart from works of the law, does not preclude the necessity of sanctification. And one of sanctification's most important constitutive elements is the daily cultivation of grateful obedience to the law. As Samuel Bolton graphically states: "The law sends us to the gospel, that we may be justified, and the gospel sends us to the law again to enquire what is our duty, being justified."[44]

Antinomians charge that those who maintain the necessity of the law as a rule of life for the believer fall prey to legalism. Now it is possible, of course, that abuse of the third use of the law can result in legalism. When an elaborate code is developed for believers to follow, covering every conceivable problem and tension in moral living, no freedom is left for believers in any area of their lives to make personal, existential decisions based on the principles of Scripture. In such a context man-made law smothers the divine gospel, and legalistic sanctification swallows up gracious justification. The Christian is then brought back into a bondage akin to that of medieval Roman Catholic monasticism.

The law affords us a comprehensive ethic, but not an exhaustive application. Scripture provides us with broad principles and illustrative paradigms, not minute particularization which can be mechanically applied to every circumstance. Daily the Christian must bring the law's broad strokes to bear on his particular decisions, carefully weighing all things according to the "law and testimony" (Isaiah 8:20) while striving and praying all the while for a growing sense of Christian prudence.

Legalism and thankful obedience to God's law operate in two radically different spheres. They differ as much from each other as do compulsory, begrudging slavery and willing, joyous service. Sadly, too many in our day confuse "law" or "legal" with "legalism" or being "legalistic." Seldom is it realized that Christ did not reject the law when He rejected legalism. Legalism is indeed a tyrant and an antagonist, but law must be our helpful and necessary friend. Legalism is a futile attempt to attain merit with God. Legalism is the error of the Pharisees: it cultivates outward conformity to the letter of the law without regard for the inward attitude of the heart.

The third use of the law steers a middle course between antinomianism and legalism. Neither antinomianism nor legalism are true to either the law or the gospel. As John Fletcher perceptively noted, "Pharisees are no more truly legal than antinomians are truly evangelical."[45] Antinomianism emphasizes Christian freedom from the condemnation of the law at the expense of the believer's pursuit of holiness. It accents justification at the expense of sanctification. It fails to see that the abrogation of the law's *condemning* power does not abrogate the law's *commanding* power. Legalism so stresses the believer's pursuit of holiness that obedience to the law becomes something more than the fruit of faith. Obedience then becomes a constituent element of justification. The commanding power of the law for sanctification all but suffocates the condemning power of the law for justification. In the final analysis, legalism denies in practice, if not in theory, a Reformed concept of justification. It accents sanctification at the expense of justification. The Reformed concept of the third use of the law helps the believer safeguard, both in doctrine and in practice, a healthy balance between justification and sanctification.[46] Justification necessarily leads to and finds its proper fruit in sanctification.[47] Salvation is by gracious faith alone, and yet cannot but produce works of grateful obedience.

Promotes Spontaneous Love

Third, the third use of the law promotes *love*. "For this is the love of God, that we keep His commandments: and His commandments are not grievous" (1 John 5:3). God's law is a gift and evidence of His tender love for His children (Psalm 147:19–20). It is not a cruel or hard taskmaster for those who are in Christ. God is no more cruel in giving His law to His own than is a farmer who builds fences to protect His cattle and horses from wandering into roads and highways. This was vividly illustrated recently in Alberta, where a horse belonging to a farmer broke through her fence, found her way to the highway and was struck by a car. Not only the horse, but also the 17-year-old driver was killed immediately. The farmer and his family wept all night. Broken fences do irreparable damage. Broken commandments reap untold consequences. But God's law, obeyed out of Spirit-worked love, promotes joy and the rejoicing of the heart. Let us thank God for His law which fences us in to contented enjoyment of the green pastures of His Word.

In Scripture law and love are not enemies, but best friends. Indeed, the essence of the law is love: "Thou shalt love the Lord thy God with all thy heart, and with all thy soul, and with all thy mind. This is the first and great commandment. And the second is like unto it, Thou shalt love thy neighbor as thyself. On these two commandments hang all the law and the prophets" (Matthew 22:37–40; cf. Romans 13:8–10). Just as a loving subject obeys his king, a loving son obeys his father, and a loving wife submits to her husband, so a loving believer yearns to obey the law of God. Then, as we have seen, the dedication of the entire Sabbath to God becomes not a burden, but a delight.

Promotes Authentic Christian Freedom

Finally, the third use of the law promotes *freedom*—genuine Christian freedom. Today's widespread abuse of the idea of Christian liberty, which is only freedom taken as an occasion to serve the flesh, should not obscure the fact that true Christian freedom is both defined and protected by the lines drawn for the believer in the law of God. Where God's law limits our freedom, it is only for our greater good; and where God's law imposes no such limits, in matters of faith and worship, the Christian enjoys perfect freedom of conscience from all the doctrines and commandments of men. In matters of daily life, true Christian freedom consists in the willing, thankful, and joyful obedience which the believer renders to God and to Christ. Calvin wrote of true Christians that they "observe the law, not as if constrained by the necessity of the law, but that freed from the law's yoke they willingly obey God's will."[48]

God's Word binds us as believers, but it binds us only to Him and His Word. He alone is Lord of our consciences. We are truly free in keeping God's commandments, for freedom flows out of grateful servitude, not out of autonomy or anarchy. We were created to love and serve God above all, and our neighbor as ourselves—all in accord with God's will and Word. Only when we realize this purpose again do we find true Christian freedom. True freedom, Calvin writes, is "a free servitude and a serving freedom." True freedom is obedient freedom. Only "those who serve God are free. We obtain liberty in order that we may more promptly and more readily obey God."[49]

> *I am, O Lord, Thy servant, bound yet free,*
> *Thy handmaid's son, whose shackles*
>   *Thou hast broken;*
> *Redeemed by grace, I'll render as a token*
> *Of gratitude my constant praise to Thee.*[50]

This, then, is the only way to live and to die. "We are God's," concludes Calvin; "let us therefore live for Him and die for Him. We are God's: let His wisdom and will therefore rule all our actions. We are God's: let all the parts of our life accordingly strive toward Him as our only lawful goal."[51]

---

[1] Psalm 119:29-32, metrical version, from *The Psalter* (1912 rpt. Grand Rapids, Mich.: Eerdmans, 1995), No. 324, verses 3–4.

[2] Many Reformed theologians, following Calvin, invert the first and second uses of the law.

[3] *Lectures on Galatians, 1535*, vol. 26 of *Luther's Works*, ed. Jeroslav Pelikan (St. Louis: Concordia, 1963), pp. 308–309.

[4] John Calvin, *Institutes of the Christian Religion*, ed. John T. McNeill, trans. Ford Lewis Battles (Philadelphia: Westminster Press, 1960), Book 2, chapter 7, paragraph 10. (hereafter, *Institutes* 2.7.10).

[5] Calvin, *Institutes* 4.20.22, 25.

6 In selecting a term for this use of the law, we are aware of the many possibilities in the literature, but have chosen the term which best expresses the Reformed view of the relationship between the law and the gospel, to wit, that they are complementary and not antithetical. Here we are dealing with that work of the law which prepares the heart of the sinner to receive Christ freely offered in the gospel to sinners as the only Savior from the law's condemnation, curse, and punishment—i.e., with evangelical rather than legal convictions. The Puritans excelled in describing this distinction, stressing that legal conviction deals only with the consequences of sin whereas evangelical conviction grapples with sin itself and the need to be delivered from it by Christ. E.g., Stephen Charnock wrote, "A legally-convinced person would only be freed from the pain [of sin], an evangelically-convinced person from the sin [itself]" (I. D. E. Thomas, *Puritan Quotations* (Chicago: Moody, 1975), p. 167).

7 The only substantial difference between Luther and Calvin on the evangelical use of the law is that for Luther this is the law's primary use, whereas for Calvin the third use of the law is primary.

8 *Luther's Works,* vol. 26, pp. 148, 150.

9 Calvin, *Institutes* 2.7.6–7.

10 *The Loci Communes of Philip Melanchthon* [1521], trans. Charles Leander Hill (Boston: Meador, 1944), p. 234.

11 *Scholia in Epistolam Pauli ad Colossense iterum ab authore recognita* (Wittenberg: J. Klug, 1534), XLVIII r, LXXXII v – LXXXIII v.

12 Ibid., XCIIII v.

13 Ibid., XVII r.

14 Ibid., XC v.

15 Ibid., L v.

16 Timothy Wengert, *Lex et Poenitentia: The Anatomy of an Early Reformation Debate Between Philip Melanchthon and John Agricola of Eisleben* (forthcoming), 303 (typewritten manuscript).

17 Wengert, *Lex et Poenitential,* p. 305.

18 *Melanchthon on Christian Doctrine (Loci communes 1555),* trans. and ed. Clyde L. Manschreck (Oxford: University Press, 1965), p.

127.
19 Cf. Hans Engelland, *Melanchthon, Glauben und Handeln* (Munich: Kaiser Verlag, 1931); Werner Elert, "Eine theologische Falschung zur Lehre vom tertius usus legis," *Zeitschrift für Religions- und Geistesgeschichte* 1 (1948):168–70; Wilfried Joest, *Gesetz und Freiheit: Das Problem des tertius usus legis bei Luther und die neutestamentliche Parainese* (Göttingen: Vandenhoeck & Ruprecht, 1951); Hayo Gerdes, *Luthers Streit mit den Schwarmern um das rechte Verständnis des Gesetzes Mose* (Göttingen: Gottiner Verlagsanstalt, 1955), 111–116; Gerhard Ebeling, *Luther: An Introduction to His Thought,* trans. R. A. Wilson (Philadelphia: Fortress, 1970); Eugene F. Klug, "Luther on Law, Gospel, and the Third Use of the Law," *The Springfielder* 38 (1974):155–69; A.C. George, "Martin Luther's Doctrine of Sanctification with Special Reference to the Formula *Simul Iustus et Peccator:* A Study in Luther's Lectures on Romans and Galatians" (Th.D. dissertation, Westminster Theological Seminary, 1982), pp. 195-210.
20 Cf. Paul Althaus, *The Theology of Martin Luther,* trans. Robert Schultz (Philadelphia: Fortress, 1966), p. 267.
21 *Luther's Works,* vol. 26, p. 260.
22 See Luther's treatises *On Good Works, The Freedom of the Christian, Small Catechism, Large Catechism,* and *Disputations with Antinomians.*
23 Cited by Donald MacLeod, "Luther and Calvin on the Place of the Law," in *Living the Christian Life* (Huntingdon, England: Westminster Conference, 1974), pp. 10–11.
24 Speaking of believers, Bucer taught that "Christ will indeed have freed [*liberasse*], but will not have loosed [*solvisse*] us from the law" (*Enarrationes* [1530], 158b; cf. 50a–51b). Francois Wendel suggests that the three functions of the law "recognized by Melanchthon" were "further accentuated by Bucer in his *Commentaries*" (*Calvin: The Origins and Development of His Religious Thought,* trans. Philip Mairet [New York: Harper & Row, 1963], 198). For example, Bucer wrote that the law "is in no sense

abolished, but is so much the more potent in each one as he is more richly endowed with the Spirit of Christ" (Wendel, *Calvin,* p. 204). Cf. Ralph Roger Sundquist, "The Third Use of the Law in the Thought of John Calvin: An Interpretation and Evaluation" (Ph.D. dissertation, Union Theological Seminary, 1970), pp. 317–18.

[25] For Calvin, the convicting use of the law is not its "proper" use, for this functioned only to drive a sinner to Christ, and the civil use was only an "accidental" purpose. Cf. Victor Shepherd, *The Nature and Function of Faith in the Theology of John Calvin* (Macon, Ga: Mercer University Press, 1983), pp. 153ff.

[26] *Selected Works of John Calvin: Tracts and Letters,* ed. Henry Beveridge and Jules Bonnet (1849; rpt. Grand Rapids, Mich.: Baker, 1983), vol. 2, pp. 56, 69.

[27] John Calvin, *Institutes of the Christian Religion:* 1536 ed., trans. Ford Lewis Battles (Grand Rapids, Mich.: Eerdmans, 1975), p. 36.

[28] *Institutes* 2.7.12. Calvin gleans considerable support for his third use of the law from the Davidic Psalms (cf. *Institutes* 2.7.12 and his *Commentary on the Book of Psalms,* trans. James Anderson, 5 vols. [Grand Rapids: Eerdmans, 1949]).

[29] I. John Hesselink, "Law—Third use of the law," in *Encyclopedia of the Reformed Faith,* ed. Donald K. McKim (Louisville, Ky.: Westminster/John Knox, 1992), pp. 215–16. Cf. Edward A. Dowey, Jr., "Law in Luther and Calvin," *Theology Today* 41, 2 (1984):146–53; I. John Hesselink, *Calvin's Concept of the Law* (Allison Park, Pa: Pickwick, 1992), pp. 251–62.

[30] *The Psalter,* No. 42.

[31] W. Robert Godfrey, "Law and Gospel," in *The New Dictionary of Theology,* ed. Sinclair B. Ferguson, David F. Wright, and J. I. Packer (Downers Grove, Ill.: InterVarsity Press, 1988), p. 379.

[32] *The Psalter,* pp. 26–88.

[33] Ernest F. Kevan, *The Grace of Law* (Pittsburgh: Soli Deo Gloria, 1990) provides a thorough treatment of Puritan teaching on the believer's relationship to the law.

[34] Anthony Burgess, *Spiritual Refining: or a Treatise of Grace and*

Assurance (London: A. Miller, 1652), p. 563.

35 Thomas Bedford, *An Examination of the chief Points of Antinomianism* (London, 1646), pp. 15–16.

36 Samuel Rutherford, *The Trial and Triumph of Faith* (Edinburgh: William Collins, 1845), p. 102; *Catechisms of the Second Reformation,* ed. Alexander F. Mitchell (London: James Nisbet, 1886), p. 226.

37 Samuel Crooke, *The Guide unto True Blessedness* (London, 1614), p. 85.

38 *Westminster Confession of Faith* (Glasgow: Free Presbyterian, 1994), 180–81.

39 *Westminster Confession of Faith,* pp. 94–95.

40 Maurice Roberts, "Sabbath Observance," *Banner of Truth,* no. 392 (May 1996) p. 5.

41 In addition to treatises on the Ten Commandments and on the Westminster Standards, see Thomas Shepard, *The Doctrine of the Sabbath* (Pittsburgh: Soli Deo Gloria, 1992); John Owen, *A n Exposition of the Epistle to the Hebrews,* ed. W. H. Goold (London: Johnstone & Hunter, 1855), vols. 3–4 on Hebrews 3–4; Jonathan Edwards, "The Perpetuity and Change of the Sabbath," in *The Works of Jonathan Edwards* (1834; rpt. Edinburgh: Banner of Truth Trust, 1974), vol. 2, pp. 93-103; Robert Dabney, "The Christian Sabbath: Its Nature, Design, and Proper Observance," in *Discussions: Evangelical and Theological* (1890; rpt. London: Banner of Truth Trust, 1967), vol. 1, pp. 496-550; Matthew Henry, "A Serious Address to Those that Profane the Lord's Day," in *The Complete Works of Matthew Henry* (1855; rpt. Grand Rapids, Mich.: Baker, 1979), vol. 1, pp. 118-133; W. B. Whitaker, *Sunday in Tudor and Stuart Times* (London: Houghton, 1933); Daniel Wilson, *The Divine Authority and Perpetual Obligation of the Lord's Day* (1827; rpt. London: Lord's Day Observance Society, 1956); John Murray, "The Moral Law and the Fourth Commandment," in *Collected Writings* (Edinburgh: Banner of Truth Trust, 1976), pp. 193-228; James I. Packer, "The Puritans and the Lord's Day," in *A Quest for*

Godliness (Wheaton: Crossway, 1990), pp. 233-43; Roger T. Beckwith and Wilfrid Stott, *The Christian Sunday: A Biblical and Historical Study* (1978; rpt. Grand Rapids, Mich.: Baker, 1980); Errol Hulse, "Sanctifying the Lord's Day: Reformed and Puritan Attitudes," in *Aspects of Sanctification* (Westminster Conference of 1981; Hertfordshire, England: Evangelical Press, 1982), pp. 78-102; James T. Dennison, Jr., *The Market Day of the Soul: The Puritan Doctrine of the Sabbath in England, 1532-1700* (New York: University Press of America, 1983); Walter Chantry, *Call the Sabbath a Delight* (Edinburgh: Banner of Truth Trust, 1991).

[42] Cf. MacLeod, "Luther and Calvin," pp. 12–13, to whom we are here indebted, for a helpful summary of observations on the normativity of the law for the believer.

[43] Cf. Psalm 119 for a remarkable example.

[44] Cited in John Blanchard, *Gathered Gold* (Welwyn, Hertfordshire, England: Evangelical Press, 1984), p. 181.

[45] "Second Check on Antinomianism," in *The Works of John Fletcher*, vol. 1, p. 338.

[46] For a more detailed description of the relationship of justification and sanctification, see Joel R. Beeke, "The Relation of Faith to Justification," in *Justification by Faith ALONE!*, ed. Don Kistler (Morgan, Pa: Soli Deo Gloria, 1995), pp. 82ff.

[47] Ernest F. Kevan, *Keep His Commandments: The Place of Law in the Christian Life* (London: Tyndale Press, 1964), p. 28.

[48] Calvin, *Institutes* 3.19.4.

[49] John Calvin, *Commentary* on 1 Peter 2:16.

[50] *The Psalter*, No. 426, verse 9 (Psalm 116).

[51] Calvin, *Institutes* 3.7.1.

Postscript

Don Kistler

For Christians, these are "the best of times and the worst of times." Never has there been such a wealth of deep, challenging Christian literature available. Never have there been more people claiming to be "born again." Yet the modern church is dangerously close to the mindset of those in Scripture who are described thus: "Every man did what was right in his own eyes" (Judges 21:25). Today, our version of that is: "Every man thinks what is right in his own mind."

For the most part, it no longer matters what centuries of church history have told us, or what centuries of diligent exegesis have yielded; today the universal hermeneutic is either "I *like* that!" or "I *don't* like that!" One's personal preference is all that matters. The issue is no longer what a passage means, but what it means to *me*! We no longer ask, "What has God said?" but "Will it work?" We have become people of consequence rather than people of conviction.

The individualism of our day (illustrated so well by the Doobie Brothers: "Me and Jesus got a good thing goin'; we don't need anyone to tell us what it's all about") has brought forth a confusion with regard to the role of obedience for the Christian. Some wish to do away with the law ("I'm not under the law, I'm under grace!"). Yet Paul wrote that the law was "holy, and righteous and good" (Romans 7:12). Why would anyone want to do away with that which was holy, righteous, and good? The true believer does not want to do away with the law any more than did Jesus, who specifically stated that He did *not* come to do away with the law, but to fulfill it. Rather, as R. C. Sproul has pointed out, the true believer, with David, *loves* God's law! It is his spiritual and moral compass. The law of God is, as the Puritans were wont to say, the character of God in transcript form.

Obedience to God and His law is the mark of a true believer. He says with David, "Thy law is my delight." He says with Christ, "I have come to do Thy will, O God." He agrees with Christ that the evidence of our love *for* Christ is our obedience *to* Christ. God desires our obedience, for in so doing we honor Him by our submission to His laws, His statutes, and His commands. Yet, as Spurgeon rightly pointed out: "He commands and receives obedience, but it is the willing obedience of the well-cared for sheep, rendered joyfully to their beloved Shepherd whose voice they know so well."

John was very clear that to obey Christ was to love Christ: "This is love, that we obey His commandments." Yet it is so important that we realize that our obedience neither contributes nor adds anything to our justification. How do you add water to a full glass? Jesus paid it *all!* Over and over again we say that obedience to Christ, our good works, prove our salvation, not bring our salvation! How could any rational person think that our imperfect works could add anything to His perfect obedience and righteousness? The great hymnwriter Horatius Bonar wrote these words to my favorite hymn:

> *Not what my hands have done*
> *Can cleanse my guilty soul*
> *Not what my toiling flesh has borne*
> *Can make my spirit whole.*
> *Not what I feel or do*
> *Can give me peace with God;*
> *Not all my prayers and sighs and tears*
> *Can bear my awful load.*
>
> *Thy work alone, O Christ,*
> *Can ease this weight of sin;*
> *Thy blood alone, O Lamb of God,*
> *Can give me peace within.*

> *Thy love to me, O God,*
> *Not mine, O Lord, to thee,*
> *Can rid me of this dark unrest,*
> *And set my spirit free.*

Or, as Augustus Toplady wrote:

> *Nothing in my hands I bring,*
> *Simply to Thy cross I cling.*

No, it is not us doing what we can and Christ doing the rest; it is Christ doing all the work of salvation and us responding with gratitude to do what He commands from hearts filled with love for His great salvation. William Secker said, "It is our bounden duty to live *in* obedience, but it would prove our utter ruin to live *on* obedience."

Jesus was quite clear in Luke 17:10 that even if we had kept all of His commands perfectly all the days of our lives, we wouldn't even deserve a "thank you." We would only have done our duty, and that would only qualify us to be unworthy, unprofitable, useless servants, according to Christ Himself! Now if perfect works deserve nothing from God, then certainly our *imperfect* works deserve even less! There is no room for anyone to think that anything we do could in any way place God under obligation to save us. Yet the Roman Catholic Church's *Canons and Decrees of the Council of Trent* tell us that "Through such good works as he does by the grace of God and the merits of Christ, whose living member he is, [a person] truly *merits* increase of grace, *eternal life*, and the attainment of eternal life if he dies in grace" (emphasis added). All of our works are stained with sin and remaining corruption and, therefore, could never merit anything at all! So Jesus taught the doctrine of "justification by faith alone" long before Luther did.

When Jesus told the story of the tax-gatherer and the Pharisee, it was the Pharisee who listed all he had done which God had indeed commanded; but it was the tax-gatherer who went home justified. This is what Paul said in Romans 4, that "to him that worketh not" is justification freely given. There he contrasts working with believing as a means of justification. No one would misunderstand him to say that someone who believes savingly into Christ will never work, but he is saying that a righteousness that is as filthy rags can never merit a perfect salvation. The imperfect can never bring the perfect, which is why faith is, of necessity, a gift of God, *not of works*. Let no one here boast!

When God has come to live in the soul of a man or woman, a boy or a girl, that person, overflowing with gratitude (Colossians 2:7), now walks in obedience to Christ. As John Mac-Arthur has said, "Obedience is now the *direction* of our life, though not the *perfection* of our life."

We sing:

> *Trust and obey, for there's no other way*
> *To be happy in Jesus, but to trust and obey.*

True as this is, it is equally true that there is no other way to be in Jesus at all! "Be ye doers of the Word and not hearers only, deceiving yourselves" (James 1:22). Do not be deceived. Judas heard all of Christ's sermons, yet he is in hell today, tormented by that which he heard and to which he failed to respond. Those who will one day see Christ are those who obey Him from the heart—not to *earn* His favor, but to *evidence* His favor.

Soli Deo Gloria!